CRACKING THE
E-COMMERCE CODE
THE BAHAMAS

Tapping into The Bahamas' Online Marketplace for Success

C. Stephan Brown &
CSB Tech Emporium

PREFACE

In an era where going digital has become the norm, **_Cracking the E-Commerce Code: The Bahamas_** is a key guide for anyone interested in online business. Authored by C. Stephan Brown & CSB Tech Emporium, this book is for those dealing in the dynamic and challenging world of e-commerce in The Bahamas.

Thanks to its distinct location and economy, The Bahamas offers a unique blend of opportunities for online businesses. Our book dives into these specifics, giving you a detailed look at how digital selling works here. We cover everything from how traditional businesses move online to the rise of online shops, selling on social media, and using mobile devices for business.

This isn't just a book about the basics of e-commerce; it's a hands-on guide to understanding and succeeding in the e-commerce sector. We will walk you through setting up your online store with easy-to-follow steps and tips to guide you through this field.

The information presented in this book is based on the e-commerce landscape in The Bahamas as of February 2024. Due to the fast-paced changes in the industry, some book details are subject to evolution. We encourage you to keep updated and adapt accordingly to maintain the relevance and effectiveness of your business strategies.

Based on what we've gathered, we've put a lot of effort into making sure the info in this book is valuable and accurate. But remember, this book is just a starting point. You need to stay informed and make smart choices for your business.

Our goal is straightforward: to equip you with the knowledge and tools necessary to succeed in The Bahamas' e-commerce field, whether you're already in business or just starting.

So, as you read through these pages, we invite you to join us on this exciting journey. Keep an open mind and be ready to explore all the possibilities the e-commerce marketplace offers. Let's start this adventure together and unlock the secrets to online business success.

C. Stephan Brown & CSB Tech Emporium

© **Copyright 2024 by C. Stephan Brown & CSB Tech Emporium - All rights reserved.**

This document is geared towards providing exact and reliable information regarding the topic and issue covered. The publication is sold with the idea that the publisher is not required to render accounting, officially permitted, or otherwise qualified services. If advice is necessary, legal, or professional, a practiced professional individual should be ordered.

- From a Declaration of Principles, which was accepted and approved equally by a Committee of the American Bar Association and a Committee of Publishers and Associations.

In no way is it legal to reproduce, duplicate, or transmit any part of this document electronically or in printed format. Recording this publication is strictly prohibited, and any storage of this document is not allowed unless with written permission from the publisher. All rights reserved.

The information provided herein is stated to be truthful and consistent in that any liability, in terms of inattention or otherwise, by any usage or abuse of any policies, processes, or directions contained within is the solitary and utter responsibility of the recipient reader. Under no circumstances will any legal responsibility or blame be held against the publisher for any reparation, damages, or monetary loss due to the information herein, either directly or indirectly.

Respective authors own all copyrights not held by the publisher.

The information herein is offered solely for informational purposes and is universal as such. The presentation of the information is without a contract or any type of guaranteed assurance.

The trademarks used are without any consent, and the trademark publication is without permission or backing by the trademark owner. All trademarks and brands within this book are for clarifying purposes only and owned by the owners themselves, not affiliated with this document.

TABLE OF CONTENTS

A GUIDE TO E-COMMERCE IN THE BAHAMAS   7

E-COMMERCE IN THE BAHAMAS   10

How E-Commerce is Transforming Business in The Bahamas   10

Benefits and Challenges of E-commerce in The Bahamas   11

CHALLENGES OF E-COMMERCE IN THE BAHAMAS   13

Current State of E-Commerce & Electronic Payment in The Bahamas   13

E-COMMERCE OPTIONS IN THE BAHAMAS   16

Online Marketplaces   16

Social Media Selling   17

Custom E-Commerce Websites   18

SETTING UP AN ONLINE STORE IN THE BAHAMAS   25

Steps for Setting Up an Online Store in The Bahamas: 26

Best Practices for Creating an Effective Online Store: 37

OVERVIEW OF E-COMMERCE PAYMENT GATEWAYS IN THE BAHAMAS	38
Different E-Commerce Payment Options Available in The Bahamas	39
HONORABLE MENTIONS	85
Vital Entities in The Bahamas' Digital Payment Ecosystem	85
BANKING INTEGRATIONS IN THE BAHAMAS	88
PAYMENT GATEWAY REFERENCE GUIDE:	92
Direct & E-Wallet Bank Integration	92
CONCLUSIONS	93
TERMINOLOGIES	95
REFERENCES	98
ABOUT THE AUTHOR	102
WHY READ CRACKING THE E-COMMERCE CODE: THE BAHAMAS?	103

A GUIDE TO E-COMMERCE IN THE BAHAMAS

Dive into The Bahamas' thriving e-commerce scene! If you're an astute entrepreneur or imaginative business owner, you no longer need a brick-and-mortar location to expand your firm. Embrace the countless openings afforded by the e-commerce revolution, allowing you to easily reach clients worldwide and propel your firm to new heights of success.

Almost every business, without exception, has reported double-digit annual growth in E-commerce. Such remarkable momentum shows no signs of abating, and it is widely anticipated that this upward trajectory will persist in the years to come.

A GUIDE TO E-COMMERCE IN THE BAHAMAS

A [recent study conducted by CBRE](#) projected that [global e-commerce sales](#) will soar to an astounding $3.9 Trillion by 2025, painting a picture of astonishing potential and limitless possibilities.

This staggering figure represents a staggering 55% growth, highlighting a monumental increase that cannot be overlooked. But here's the exciting part - even The Bahamas is poised to contribute to this meaningful growth, carving its own path in the world of E-commerce sales.

The Rise of E-Commerce and The Bahamas' Potential

PROJECTED GLOBAL SALES

A recent study by CBRE projects that global e-commerce sales will reach a staggering $3.9 Trillion (USD) by 2025, reflecting the industry's extraordinary potential.

This projection represents an astonishing 55% growth, emphasizing the monumental increase and opportunities in the e-commerce landscape potential.

Even The Bahamas is poised to join this monumental growth, carving its path in e-commerce sales and expanding its presence on the global stage.

As more people worldwide turn to online shopping, it's no surprise that the e-commerce industry is growing rapidly.

With the convenience of shopping from the comfort of your home and the ability to compare prices and products easily, e-commerce is quickly becoming the go-to choose for many consumers.

So, whether you're a Bahamian entrepreneur looking to expand your reach or a customer looking for the convenience of online shopping, the growing e-commerce market is something to keep an eye on.

This guide is designed to help you navigate the exciting world of e-commerce in The Bahamas. We will explore the current state of e-commerce in the country and the various options available to businesses looking to establish an online presence. Whether you are interested in setting up your online store or simply want to explore the different e-commerce payment systems available in The Bahamas, this guide has got you covered.

Get ready to take your business or shopping experience to the next level by embracing the future of commerce. Keep reading to find out more!

E-COMMERCE IN THE BAHAMAS

How E-Commerce is Transforming Business in The Bahamas

Well, well, well, it looks like the tides are turning for businesses in The Bahamas, thanks to the rise of e-commerce! Can you believe that businesses used to be limited to physical locations and local customers only? But now, with the power of e-commerce, businesses can spread their wings and reach customers beyond their wildest dreams.

Imagine being a small business owner in The Bahamas and being able to compete with larger businesses on a level playing field. That's what e-commerce has made possible! It's allowed small businesses to expand their reach and tap into the global market. No longer are they confined to the local market; they can now compete on a much larger scale.

And let's not forget how e-commerce has revolutionized how businesses communicate with their target customers. Social media platforms have become critical for businesses to reach and engage with customers. E-commerce platforms have made it easier for businesses to manage customer relationships and provide top-notch customer service. With e-commerce, businesses can now create a more personalized experience for their customers, building stronger relationships and increasing customer loyalty.

It's no surprise that e-commerce has become increasingly popular in The Bahamas.

According to a recent survey, more than 60% of consumers in The Bahamas have made an online purchase in the past year, and business owners are taking notice, too! More and more businesses are establishing an online presence, with 35% of businesses in the country already having an online store or website.

The Commonwealth of The Bahamas has also demonstrated its interest in the e-commerce business by implementing various [Bills, Acts, and Policies](#) to regulate e-commerce activity within the country.

It's clear that e-commerce is changing the game for businesses in The Bahamas. The possibilities are endless, and it's exciting to see how businesses adapt and thrive in this new era of commerce.

Who knows what the future holds? One thing's for sure: With e-commerce, the sky's the limit!

Benefits and Challenges of E-commerce in The Bahamas

E-commerce in The Bahamas comes with both benefits and challenges. Let's take a closer look at each:

Benefits of E-Commerce in The Bahamas

Increased Reach: E-commerce allows businesses to reach customers beyond their geographical location, expanding their customer base and increasing their sales potential.

Cost Savings: By operating online, businesses can reduce the overhead costs associated with a physical store, such as rent and utilities.

Increased Efficiency: E-commerce platforms provide businesses with tools to manage their operations more efficiently, including inventory management, order processing, and customer relationship management.

Increased Competition: E-commerce provides businesses of all sizes with a level playing field, allowing smaller businesses to compete with larger businesses.

CHALLENGES OF E-COMMERCE IN THE BAHAMAS

Logistics: Shipping and logistics can be challenging for businesses in The Bahamas, as the country has over 700 islands, many of which are remote and difficult to access.

Payment Processing: Payment processing can be a challenge for businesses in The Bahamas, as many e-commerce platforms do not support Bahamian currency, and international payment processors often charge high fees. We shall discuss some common payment gateways available in The Bahamas. So, keep tuned, and I'll give you a rundown of what's available.

Despite these challenges, e-commerce is still growing in this Lucayan Archipelago, and businesses have many opportunities to take advantage of this trend.

In the next section, we'll explore the different e-commerce options in The Bahamas, so keep your eyes peeled!

Current State of E-Commerce & Electronic Payment in The Bahamas

The e-commerce landscape in The Bahamas is still relatively new but growing rapidly. According to a [2020 report by the Central Bank of The Bahamas](#), the value of electronic retail transactions in The Bahamas increased by 10.3% from 2019 to 2020, with the total value of electronic retail transactions reaching $470.4 million in 2020.

CHALLENGES OF E-COMMERCE IN THE BAHAMAS

The report also notes that the COVID-19 pandemic accelerated the growth of e-commerce in The Bahamas, as many businesses had to pivot to online sales to survive during the pandemic. As a result, many businesses have started to adopt e-commerce platforms, and there has been an increase in the number of e-commerce businesses in the country.

A recent revelation from The Central Bank of The Bahamas (CBOB) showed that people continually embrace the ever-growing realm of electronic payments.

According to the [CBOB's 2022 Annual Report](), the year witnessed an impressive surge in electronic transactions, primarily driven by a remarkable 18 percent upswing in debit card usage. This substantial growth exemplified the populace's inclination towards leveraging credit cards, debit cards, and automated cash dispensing services, thereby minimizing reliance on credit finance transactions. These significant shifts also encapsulated a resurgence in consumer spending, recovering from the downturn experienced during the pandemic's grip, specifically, regarding card-based payments, the volume of debit card transactions escalated by an impressive 18.2 percent, totaling 20.8 million transactions, accompanied by a 16.6 percent increase in value, reaching a staggering $2.3 billion.

Furthermore, the report elaborates on the expanding number of credit cards in circulation. In 2022, the number of credit cards issued or renewed by commercial banks experienced a notable 4.9 percent growth, resulting in 95,049 cards.

Concurrently, the overall outstanding debt associated with these credit cards also saw a modest rise of 2.0 percent, amounting to $221.2 million.

Remarkably, the volume of purchases and other credit transactions, most of which were repaid within the same period, witnessed a remarkable rebound of 27.5 percent, accumulating to a total value of $1.2 billion. However, despite this significant recovery, credit card transactions remained below the pre-pandemic levels due to a notable shift towards debit card usage.

These latest insights reflect the ongoing transformation in the financial landscape of The Bahamas, with residents embracing the convenience, security, and efficiency offered by electronic transactions for e-commerce. As the archipelago continues its journey towards a cashless society, the progressive adoption of electronic payment methods demonstrates the nation's resilience and adaptability in the face of unprecedented challenges.

Despite this growth, there is still a long way to go for e-commerce in The Bahamas. Many businesses are still not fully embracing e-commerce, and challenges, such as internet connectivity and logistics, must be overcome. However, with the increasing popularity of e-commerce and the growing demand for online shopping, the future of e-commerce in The Bahamas looks bright.

E-COMMERCE OPTIONS IN THE BAHAMAS

The Bahamas is home to several e-commerce options, each with its own advantages and disadvantages.

In this section, we'll take a closer look at the different e-commerce options available in the country and provide an overview of each one.

Online Marketplaces

Online marketplaces are one of the most popular e-commerce options in The Bahamas. These platforms allow businesses to set up an online store and sell their products to customers through a trusted and established website.

According to a report by Statista, the number of digital buyers in The Bahamas is expected to reach approximately 156,000 by 2024. This presents an excellent opportunity for businesses to reach a wider audience by leveraging the existing customer base on online marketplaces.

By 2021, the online marketplace witnessed an exponential surge as more than 2.14 billion individuals across the globe embraced the convenience of purchasing goods and services digitally. This staggering figure marks a significant increase from the 1.66 billion global digital buyers recorded in 2016, underscoring the widespread adoption and growing popularity of online transactions.

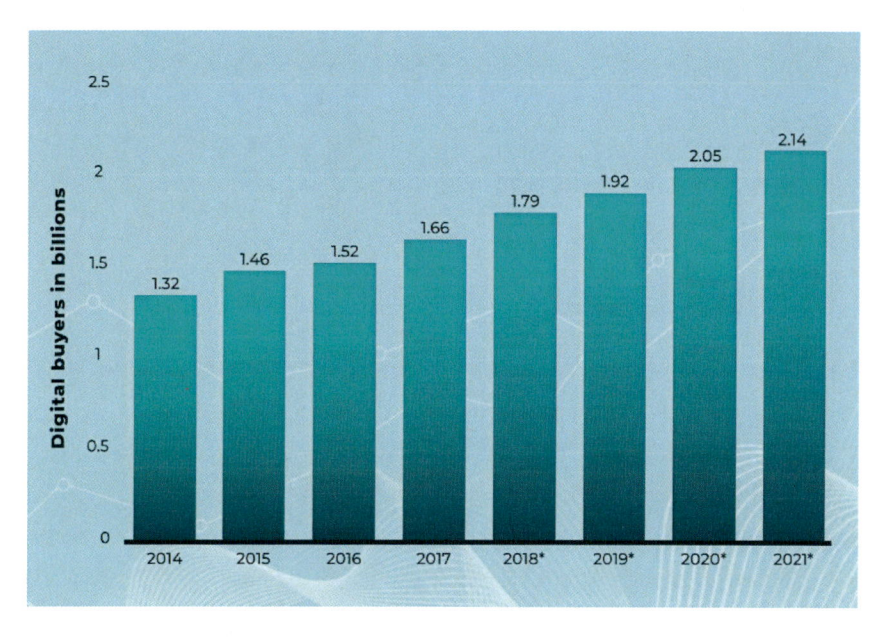

The presented timeline comprehensively illustrates the global digital buyer population from 2014 to 2021.

Social Media Selling

Social media selling is another popular e-commerce option in The Bahamas. According to a 2022 report by Hootsuite, approximately 85% of the population in The Bahamas uses social media, presenting a vast potential customer base for businesses. Setting up a business page on social media platforms, such as Facebook and Instagram, is relatively easy and requires minimal setup costs.

One of the benefits of social media selling is that businesses can engage with customers directly, building relationships and increasing customer loyalty. Social media platforms also offer built-in marketing tools, making it easier for businesses to promote their products.

However, businesses that use social media for selling must compete with other businesses and content on these platforms, making it difficult to stand out. Additionally, social media platforms can be unpredictable, as changes in algorithms and policies can affect the visibility of businesses' posts.

Custom E-Commerce Websites

Custom e-commerce websites are online stores built from scratch, giving businesses complete control over their store's design, functionality, and user experience. This option offers businesses more flexibility and control over the online shopping experience than other e-commerce options like online marketplaces or social media selling.

One of the main benefits of custom e-commerce websites is the ability to fully customize the design and functionality of the online store, creating a unique and personalized shopping experience for customers. This allows businesses to differentiate themselves from competitors and build a strong brand identity. Additionally, custom e-commerce websites offer businesses more control over their customer data, which can be used to create targeted marketing campaigns and improve customer engagement.

However, building and maintaining a custom e-commerce website can be costly and time-consuming. A business site should be secure and user-friendly, which can be complex. Custom e-commerce websites require more upfront investment and ongoing maintenance costs, which can be a barrier for small businesses.

Regardless of these constraints, custom e-commerce websites offer businesses the ability to build a unique online store that reflects their brand identity and business goals. These websites can be designed to be user-friendly, intuitive, easy to navigate, optimized for conversions, and provide a positive user experience for customers.

Businesses can also add specific features and functionality to their website, such as custom search filters, product comparison tools, and personalized recommendations. This makes the shopping experience more personalized and tailored to customers' needs.

Building and maintaining a custom e-commerce website is made significantly easier with the integration of Content Management Systems (CMS). These programs are instrumental in simplifying the complexities associated with digital store management, reducing both the cost and effort involved.

You might be curious about what a CMS is. Don't worry; in the next sections, we'll learn more about CMS solutions and check out the different available options to improve your online store.

To summarize, custom e-commerce websites can be an excellent option for businesses that want more control over their online store and are willing to invest in creating a unique and personalized shopping experience for their customers.

Content Management Systems (CMS)

Managing an effective e-commerce webpage is possible with a Content Management System (CMS). A CMS is a software application or related group of programs used to create and manage digital content. These platforms let businesses easily update and handle their website's content and features.

For a highly personalized online store, a developer can craft a custom CMS to cater to the distinct needs of a business website. This includes tailored workflows, data organization, aesthetic preferences, and how users interact with the site.

This approach not only makes your website shop unique and competitive but also helps it adapt to the sales goals.

CMS PLATFORMS

WooCommerce

An extension of WordPress, WooCommerce is a powerful, open-source e-commerce plugin that enables businesses to transform their websites into versatile online stores. It's celebrated for its user-friendly interface, extensive customization options, and robust functionality, including various payment gateway integrations and scalable solutions for businesses of all sizes.

Magento

Magento stands out for its open-source technology, providing online merchants with a flexible shopping cart system, control over the look, content, and functionality of your online store, and a suite of powerful tools for marketing, search engine optimization, and catalog management. Ideal for businesses seeking a scalable platform, Magento supports extensive customization and integration capabilities.

Joomla

Joomla is a free, open-source CMS for publishing web content. It's designed to be easy to install and set up, even if you're not an advanced user. Joomla is highly extensible, and thousands of extensions and templates are available to customize a site to fit your needs. It's suitable for building web applications, websites, and powerful online applications. Joomla offers features such as page caching, RSS feeds, printable versions of pages, news flashes, blogs, search, and support for language internationalization.

Shopify

Shopify is recognized for its comprehensive tools that simplify the creation and management of an online store. A hosted solution, it removes the complexity of technical setup, making it accessible for entrepreneurs to focus on their business. Shopify's strength lies in its ease of use, extensive app marketplace, and reliable customer support.

BigCommerce

A cloud-based e-commerce solution, BigCommerce is designed for businesses aiming for growth without the hassle of complex technical requirements. It offers a wide array of built-in features, customization options, and scalability, catering to the needs of expanding online stores.

Wix

Known for its simplicity, Wix is a user-friendly platform that allows for the quick creation of e-commerce sites through a drag-and-drop interface. It's best suited for small businesses and individual entrepreneurs looking for an easy-to-use solution with basic e-commerce capabilities.

Mobile Commerce

Mobile commerce, also known as m-commerce, is a growing trend in The Bahamas. This involves selling products through mobile devices such as smartphones and tablets. Mobile commerce can take many forms, such as mobile apps, mobile-optimized websites, and text message marketing. With most Bahamians owning a smartphone, mobile commerce presents a vast opportunity for businesses to reach a broad and engaged audience.

There are several ways in which businesses can engage in mobile commerce, including mobile apps, mobile-optimized websites, and text message marketing.

Mobile apps are an excellent option for businesses that want to create a seamless shopping experience for their customers, as they can offer features such as push notifications and personalized recommendations.

Interestingly, the development of these apps is increasingly relying on Cross-Platform Development Tools, which allow for their deployment across multiple mobile operating systems, thus broadening the potential customer base.

This approach is particularly relevant for mobile commerce, as it ensures that businesses can cater to all smartphone users, regardless of their device.

Mobile-optimized websites are another option that allows businesses to optimize their website for smaller screens and touch-based interactions. Similarly, text message marketing can send promotions and alerts directly to customers' phones. One of the main benefits of mobile commerce is that it allows businesses to reach customers wherever they are.

Customers can easily browse and purchase from their mobile devices, increasing engagement and sales. Additionally, mobile commerce can offer businesses valuable customer data, which can be used to create targeted marketing campaigns and improve customer engagement.

However, there are also some challenges associated with mobile commerce. One of the main challenges is ensuring that the mobile shopping experience is user-friendly and easy to navigate. Mobile devices have smaller screens and different input methods than desktop computers, making it difficult for businesses to create a seamless shopping experience.

Additionally, businesses must ensure that their mobile commerce solutions are secure and can protect customers' personal and financial information.

Cross-platform development tools not only address challenges by facilitating the creation of adaptable and user-friendly mobile applications but also enhance security across different platforms. This technological strategy is pivotal for businesses aiming to harness the full potential of mobile commerce.

Nonetheless, mobile commerce presents a massive opportunity for businesses in The Bahamas. With most Bahamians owning a smartphone, companies that invest in mobile commerce can reach a large and engaged audience, creating a seamless shopping experience for their customers.

CROSS-PLATFORM DEVELOPMENT TOOLS

React Native
A framework for building native mobile apps using JavaScript and React, React Native facilitates the development of applications for both iOS and Android from a single codebase, promoting efficiency and cohesiveness across platforms.

Flutter
Developed by Google, Flutter is an open-source UI software development kit used for creating natively compiled applications for mobile, web, and desktop from a single codebase using Dart. It's known for its fast development cycle, expressive and flexible UI, and native performance.

Xamarin

Xamarin, a Microsoft-owned framework, allows developers to create native apps for Android, iOS, and Windows using a single, shared C# codebase. It emphasizes code sharing across platforms, making it a cost-effective solution for developing cross-platform applications.

SETTING UP AN ONLINE STORE IN THE BAHAMAS

Setting up an online store in The Bahamas can be daunting. Still, it can be a rewarding and profitable endeavor with the right approach and tools.

We will go through the steps for setting up an online store in The Bahamas and share best practices that may guide you in creating an effective online store.

Steps for Setting Up an Online Store in The Bahamas:

Choose your e-commerce platform

The first step in setting up an online store is choosing the right e-commerce platform for your business. As discussed earlier, various options are available, including online marketplaces, social media selling, custom e-commerce websites, and mobile commerce. Consider the needs of your business, the size of your inventory, and your budget before making a decision.

Register your business in The Bahamas

Before launching your online store, you must register your business with the relevant authorities in The Bahamas. Below are the steps that would assist you in registering your business:

SETTING UP AN ONLINE STORE IN THE BAHAMAS

Step 1: Choose the Right Business Entity

Begin by selecting the appropriate business entity for your venture. Options include an International Business Company (IBC), a Domestic Company, or an Exempted Limited Partnership. This choice should be based on your business activities, tax considerations, and the nationalities of shareholders and directors.

Step 2: Name Reservation

To secure the desired name for your business, you must reserve it through the [Registrar General's Department](). This is a vital step in confirming the availability of your chosen business name and securing it for your exclusive use. Before proceeding with the name reservation, it's important to register an account on the [Bahamas Government Portal.]() This online portal facilitates the process, allowing you to manage and track your application conveniently.

Step 3: Prepare Supporting Documents

Gather and prepare all necessary documents, such as identification proofs and names of directors. You must also draft and notarize your company's Memorandum and Articles of Association.

Step 4: Company Registration

File your prepared documents with the Registrar General's Department. Ensure you have a registered office and an agent within The Bahamas, as these are required for registration.

Step 5: Open a Corporate Bank Account

Once your company is registered, open a corporate bank account. Depending on your business needs, this can be done with either local or offshore banks.

STEP 6: OBTAIN BUSINESS LICENSES

In The Bahamas, all new or existing businesses must have a business license according to the Business License Act, 2023. If you're incorporating a company, registering it is a vital legal requirement to comply with local laws. This is an essential step in establishing a business in The Bahamas.

1. Begin by filling out the business license application form, starting with registering your business name. If your chosen name is rejected, you will be notified and asked to select an alternative from your previously submitted options.

2. Once you have completed the application, the Business License Unit will contact you to inform you when your license is ready for collection.

SUPPORTING DOCUMENTS:

- **Certificate of Incorporation:** Provide a copy of the current annual company payment receipt.

- **National Insurance:** Submit a current letter of good standing from the National Insurance Board and the applicant's National Insurance Board Card.

- **Proof of Business Location:** Include a copy of the lease, rental agreement, or proof of ownership. Also, approvals should be obtained from departments like Physical Planning, Ministry of Works/Building Control, and Environmental Health Services.

- **Real Property Tax Payment:** If applicable, show proof of payment for property taxes for the location where the business is situated.

TURN-AROUND TIME:
Applications are generally processed within seven working days following the submission and approval of the business name. Learn more details on [The Official Website of the Government of The Bahamas.](#)

FEES:
A license fee of BS$ 100.00 is required for new businesses. Payment can be made by certified cheque, cash, or credit card.

STEP 7: FINANCIAL REPORTING AND TAXATION

Register for taxation and familiarize yourself with your tax obligations in The Bahamas. Note that International Business Companies (IBCs) are exempt from certain taxes like income, capital gains, or estate tax but may still be liable for value-added tax on some goods and services.

ACCOUNTING AND TAX OBLIGATIONS
Stay compliant with annual reporting requirements.

ADDITIONAL INFORMATION
The Bahamas offers various business entities, including the popular International Business Company (IBC), known for its minimal requirements and tax exemptions.

Try visiting these pages on The Bahamas Government's website (https://www.bahamas.gov.bs) for more detailed information:

- Bahamas Investment Authority
- Registrar General's Department
- Ministry of Finance's Business License Unit

Choose your domain name

Your domain name is your website address and is an important part of your brand identity. Choose a domain name that is easy to remember, relevant to your business, and reflects your brand identity.

Design your website

One of the big factors that may attract and create a positive user experience for your customers is the design of your website. Choose a design that is visually appealing, easy to navigate, and optimized for mobile devices.

Set up your payment gateway

A secure and reliable payment gateway is also needed for accepting customer payments. Choose a payment gateway that is widely used and trusted, and ensure it complies with PCI DSS (Payment Card Industry Data Security Standard).

1. UNDERSTAND THE PAYMENT ECOSYSTEM

Familiarize yourself with the roles of key players like the customer, merchant, payment gateway, payment processor, and acquiring bank. This understanding is necessary in choosing the right gateway type for your needs.

2. CHOOSE A PAYMENT GATEWAY OR DO A SELF-BUILD

Decide whether to use a third-party payment gateway or self-build your own. Let's know the difference between these two:

- **THIRD-PARTY PAYMENT GATEWAYS:**
  Opting for a third-party payment gateway means choosing an easy-to-use, pre-set service. It's ideal for those who prefer simplicity and minimal technical involvement.

  Plus, integrating your chosen gateway would be easier with CSB Tech. We help integrate these gateways seamlessly with your website, ensuring a smooth operation. So, Third-Party Payment Gateways are an excellent choice for hassle-free online payment handling.

- **SELF-BUILD PAYMENT GATEWAYS:**
  On the other hand, building your own payment gateway gives you complete control. It's perfect for businesses with unique needs that standard options don't cover, allowing for customized features. However, it demands considerable technical know-how, as you'll manage everything from security to system upkeep.

3. APPLY FOR A MERCHANT ACCOUNT

Your chosen gateway provider will assist you in applying for a merchant account with an acquiring bank. This account is essential for accepting payments and receiving funds.

4. INTEGRATE THE GATEWAY WITH YOUR WEBSITE

Integrate the gateway's Application Programming Interfaces (API) with your website's checkout process. This may involve modifying your website code or using provided plugins or extensions.

For WooCommerce users, CSB Tech offers specialized plugins like SunCash, First Atlantic Commerce, and Cash N Go, enhancing the functionality and user experience of your e-commerce platform. Alongside these mentioned plugins, we have other plugins at CSB Tech's Online Shop, ready for immediate use.

5. Configure Features and Settings

Set up your preferred payment methods, currencies, fraud prevention tools, and other features the gateway offers. CSB Tech can assist in configuring these settings to match your specific business requirements.

6. Test and Refine

Thoroughly test your checkout process and payment flow to ensure smooth functionality and a positive user experience. This includes testing different payment methods, error scenarios, and mobile responsiveness.

7. Launch and Monitor

Once everything is functioning properly, launch your website and start accepting payments. Monitor transaction logs for any issues or suspicious activity.

Additional Points to Consider

- **Security and Compliance:** Ensure your chosen gateway meets industry security standards like PCI DSS.
- **Tech and Service Support:** Choose a payment gateway with solid service support, complemented by CSB Tech's expert integration services for a straightforward setup and troubleshooting.
- **Transaction Fees and Pricing:** Understand the fee structure of your chosen gateway and ensure it aligns with your budget.
- **Scalability:** Choose a gateway that can scale with your business growth.

Create your product listings

Creating a detailed and accurate product listing is a huge puzzle piece of setting up your online store. A well-crafted product listing may turn potential interest into actual customer commitment.

Include high-quality images, detailed descriptions, and pricing information for each product.

Set up shipping and delivery options

Local shipping in The Bahamas presents distinct challenges compared to other compact countries, primarily due to its unique geographical and logistical landscape.

The archipelago comprises over 700 islands, necessitating complex and often costly inter-island transportation, unlike the more straightforward mainland routes in the United States. This may often lead to longer delivery times and higher costs.

So, providing fast and reliable shipping options is crucial in meeting your customers' expectations. Choose a reliable shipping provider and offer various delivery options to meet your customers' needs.

Here's a more detailed Bahamian shipping process:

SETTING UP AN ONLINE STORE IN THE BAHAMAS

1. **PRODUCT PREPARATION**
   When preparing a product for shipping in The Bahamas, it's essential to ensure the item is safely packaged using sturdy boxes and protective materials like bubble wrap.

   Additionally, the package should be clearly labeled with the recipient's address and contact information. For international shipments, including a return address and the necessary customs documentation is crucial to facilitate smooth transit and avoid any customs-related delays.

2. **CHOOSING A SHIPPING SERVICE**
   For shipping within The Bahamas, selecting a local courier or shipping service specializing in inter-island deliveries is advisable. However, for international shipping needs, opting for well-known services such as FedEx, DHL, UPS, or a local company that provides international shipping options would be more appropriate. This choice largely depends on the destination and the nature of the goods being shipped.

3. **CUSTOMS DOCUMENTATION (FOR INTERNATIONAL SHIPPING)**
   For international shipping, completing all required customs forms accurately is important. These forms should detail the contents of the package and their value. Proper documentation is key to preventing delays in customs and ensuring a smooth delivery process across borders.

4. **DROP-OFF OR PICKUP**

   Regarding the physical handling of the package, there are two main options. One can either drop off the package at a local point designated by the chosen courier or shipping service or, if available, opt for a pickup service where the courier comes to your location to collect the package. The latter can often be scheduled in advance for added convenience.

5. **PAYMENT AND SHIPPING OPTIONS**

   When it comes to payment and choosing shipping options, decisions should be based on the urgency of the delivery and the budget at hand. Options typically include standard, express, or overnight shipping, with costs varying according to the package's size, weight, destination, and delivery speed.

6. **TRACKING AND UPDATES**

   Most shipping services offer a tracking number, allowing the sender and the recipient to monitor the package's progress. This feature is particularly important for international shipments, which may take longer and require passage through customs. Keeping the recipient informed about the shipment's status is a good practice to ensure transparency and manage expectations.

SETTING UP AN ONLINE STORE IN THE BAHAMAS

DELIVERY OPTIONS IN THE BAHAMAS

- **Standard Shipping:** In The Bahamas, standard shipping is the regular delivery service and is typically the most cost-effective option. This method is best suited for non-urgent deliveries where time is not critical.

- **Express Shipping:** Express Shipping offers a faster delivery solution, usually at a higher cost. This option is ideal for urgent or time-sensitive shipments where speed is a priority.

- **Air Freight:** This option is mostly used for quicker delivery between the islands or international shipping. While more expensive, it is significantly faster than sea transport, making it a preferred choice for time-sensitive deliveries.

- **Sea Freight:** This option is common for transporting heavy or bulky items. It is more economical than air freight but has a slower transit time. This option suits large shipments where cost efficiency is more important than speed.

- **Door-to-Door Delivery:** Some couriers in The Bahamas offer comprehensive door-to-door delivery services. This includes pickup from the sender's location and direct delivery to the recipient's doorstep, providing convenience and a complete shipping solution.

- **Customized Solutions:** Some shipping companies in The Bahamas provides customized solutions. These can include specialized services like refrigerated shipping for perishable goods and catering to specific requirements of unique items.

Best Practices for Creating an Effective Online Store:

- **Optimize your website for search engines:** Search engine optimization (SEO) is another variable in driving traffic to your website. Ensure that your website is optimized for relevant keywords and that your product listings are optimized for search engines.

- **Create a strong brand identity:** Create a strong brand identity, this would build customer trust and loyalty to your services or products. Ensure your website design, logo, and marketing materials consistently reflect your brand identity.

- **Offer excellent customer service:** Excellent customer service stands out as the primary factor that shapes your entire business. Aim to build positive customer relationships. Respond to inquiries and complaints promptly and professionally and provide a clear and easy-to-understand return policy.

- **Promote your online store:** Promoting your online store is a must to attract new customers and grow your business. Use social media, email marketing, and other online marketing channels to promote your products and attract new customers.

Setting up an online store in The Bahamas requires careful planning and execution. By following the steps outlined above and implementing best practices for creating an effective online store, you can create a successful e-commerce business and reach a wider audience of customers.

OVERVIEW OF E-COMMERCE PAYMENT GATEWAYS IN THE BAHAMAS

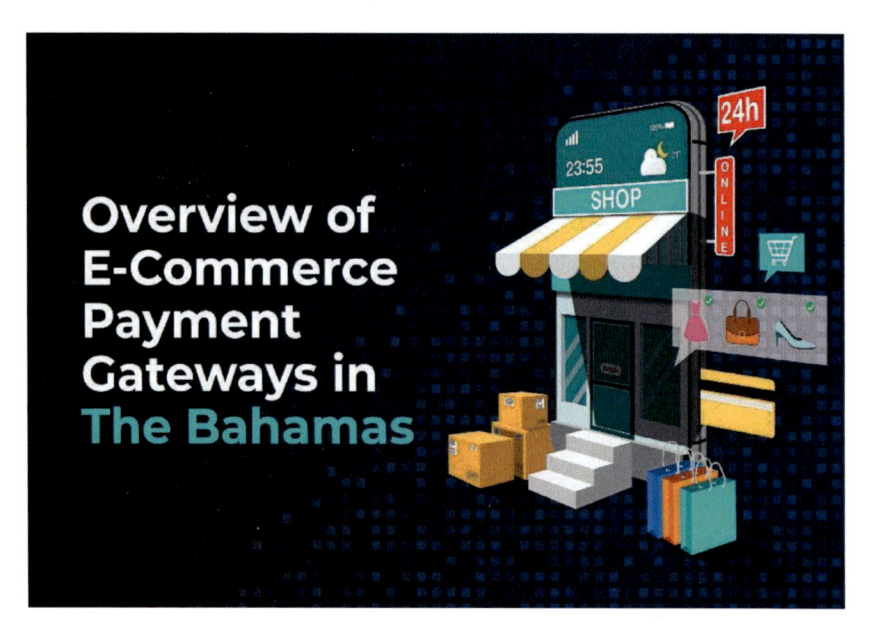

An e-commerce payment gateway is a technology that enables online transactions by securely processing customers' credit card or debit card information. Payment gateways are essential for any business that operates an online store, as they provide a secure means for customers to pay for products and services.

OVERVIEW OF E-COMMERCE PAYMENT GATEWAYS IN THE BAHAMAS

Different E-Commerce Payment Options Available in The Bahamas

In The Bahamas, several e-commerce payment gateway options are available for businesses.

BlueSnap

BlueSnap is a global payment gateway that enables businesses to accept payments from customers worldwide. It offers various payment processing solutions, including credit and debit cards, e-wallets, bank transfers, and more. An important aspect to note for businesses considering BlueSnap is the specific merchant requirements: the service is available to businesses with an established presence in the EU, UK, US, AUS, or LATAM, and they must process a minimum of $50,000 per month.

BlueSnap can handle transactions in the Bahamas and in local currency, but this requires a secondary entity for underwriting purposes.

Let's take a closer look at BlueSnap's main features, pricing, and how it integrates with other systems.

FEATURES:

- **Fraud prevention:** BlueSnap offers advanced fraud prevention tools to protect merchants from chargebacks and fraudulent transactions.

- **Subscription billing:** Merchants can set up recurring payments for subscriptions, memberships, and other ongoing services using BlueSnap's subscription billing feature.

- **PCI compliance:** BlueSnap is fully PCI compliant, which means it meets the strict security standards required by the credit card industry to protect cardholder data.

- **Mobile optimization:** BlueSnap offers mobile-optimized checkout pages, allowing customers to easily make payments from their smartphones and tablets.

- **Customizable Payment Forms:** Users can create and customize payment forms to suit their branding needs. This feature enables users to modify the design of the payment forms to match their website or application, providing an integrated checkout experience for their customers.

- **Payment Analytics:** This feature provides users with in-depth analytics on their payment processes. Giving insights into payment success rates, average transaction values, and other essential metrics that could help businesses make informed decisions about their payment strategies.

- **Recurring Payments:** Users can set up recurring payments for subscriptions, memberships, or other recurring billing services. This feature allows customers to automatically pay for products or services regularly, increasing customer retention and revenue.

- **Mobile Point of Sale (mPOS):** This feature allows businesses to process payments on the go using a mobile device. This enables businesses to accept customer payments in person, at events, or on the street.

- **Automated Accounts Receivable:** BlueSnap's solution provides automated accounts receivable, making it easier for businesses to manage their cash flow.

- **Virtual Terminal:** This component enables enterprises to handle telephonic or electronic mail transactions. It ensures businesses can receive payments from patrons lacking the necessary capabilities or resources for standard payment methods.

- **All-in-One Payment Orchestration Platform:** BlueSnap's modular solution offers everything businesses need to sell globally, from online and mobile checkout to subscriptions, virtual terminals, and invoice payments.

- **Automated Fraud and Chargeback Management:** With built-in fraud and chargeback management solutions, BlueSnap helps businesses reduce their risk of fraud and chargebacks.

- **Built-in Solutions for Regulation and Tax Compliance:** BlueSnap's solution includes built-in solutions for regulation and tax compliance, making it easier for businesses to comply with regulations in different countries.

- **Reporting:** BlueSnap's solution provides reporting to increase visibility and simplify reconciliation.

OVERVIEW OF E-COMMERCE PAYMENT GATEWAYS IN THE BAHAMAS

PRICING:

Bluesnap is an all-in-one payment orchestration platform that offers flexible payment processing solutions for businesses of all sizes. They provide customized pricing solutions for established businesses with large payment volumes or unique business needs and a Quick Start Pricing plan for businesses without a prior payment processing history. With Bluesnap, you can process payments globally using a single account.

Customized Pricing:

This plan suits established businesses with large payment volumes or unique business needs. Bluesnap offers a pricing solution that is tailored to your business needs. There is no setup, cancellation, or additional fees for e-wallets. The pricing model can be interchanged plus, tiered, or flat-rate pricing, and there are Level 2 and Level 3 data processing rates. There are special payment processing rates if you're a charity or nonprofit. Additionally, the plan offers accounts receivable automation.

Quick Start Pricing:

This plan is suitable for businesses without prior payment processing history or statements. With the Quick Start Pricing plan, you can start with simple pay-as-you-go pricing. However, this plan does not apply to high-risk merchants. Bluesnap suggests custom pricing so those merchants can get the most from their payments.

Bluesnap offers global processing with one account, and you can choose your preferred pricing plan based on your business needs.

OVERVIEW OF E-COMMERCE PAYMENT GATEWAYS IN THE BAHAMAS

INTEGRATION OPTIONS:

Integrated with the Software You Already Use: BlueSnap's payment solution works with hundreds of business platforms, such as shopping carts, ERP & CRM (Customer Relationship Management) systems, and more.

Embedded Payments and Payfac-as-a-Service: With BlueSnap, businesses can own the payment experience for their clients and choose the branding, payment flow, and payouts.
The technology supports global payments with expedited onboarding, international compliance, and ongoing program management.

Overall, BlueSnap is a robust payment gateway solution with many features and customization options. Its multi-currency support and advanced fraud prevention tools make it a particularly strong choice for businesses that sell internationally. However, the pricing model can be complex and unsuitable for small businesses or those with low transaction volumes.

Cash N' Go Merchant Services & Cash Management Solutions

[Cash N' Go Merchant Services](#) provides a versatile and comprehensive suite of tools designed to empower businesses in The Bahamas, offering various avenues to manage payments and enhance revenue streams. This service streamlines how companies can interact with customers through multiple payment channels, whether online, mobile applications, or virtual terminals.

OVERVIEW OF E-COMMERCE PAYMENT GATEWAYS IN THE BAHAMAS

FEATURES:

- **Multiple Payment Channels:** Accept payments through different mediums, ensuring businesses can cater to a broader customer base.

- **Integration with Sand Dollar:** Incorporates the Sand Dollar payment system, allowing for seamless digital currency transactions.

- **Real-Time Processing:** Payments are processed in real-time, offering instant access to funds for various uses like utility payments, salary disbursements, and bank transfers.

- **Secure Platform:** Emphasizes security with a secured merchant platform, giving businesses and their customers peace of mind.

- **Direct API Integration:** Connects easily with business websites through direct API integration for online payments.

- **Accessibility:** Funds collected are immediately accessible and manageable through the Cash N' Go Merchant Administrator Portal.

- **Cash Management:** Physical locations across several islands provide the convenience of depositing cash sales directly into merchant accounts.

- **Marketing Opportunities:** Offers in-app advertising, potentially increasing brand visibility among over 15,000 Cash N' Go mobile app users.

OVERVIEW OF E-COMMERCE PAYMENT GATEWAYS IN THE BAHAMAS

PRICING:

No Start-Up or Monthly Subscription Fees: The service eliminates upfront costs, allowing businesses to sign up for free.

Transaction-Based Fees: Businesses pay fees based on the transactions processed:

- **Cash Deposit Fee:** Ranges from $2.00 per deposit to 0.75% of the deposit amount, based on monthly aggregate amounts.

- **Bank Transfers:** A flat fee of $10.00 per transfer to any local bank.

- **In-Network Transfers:** A nominal $0.15 per transfer, with batch disbursements at $5.00 per batch.

- **Merchant Fee:** A 4% fee per transaction for card payments processed through the merchant terminal.

HOW TO GET STARTED WITH CASH N' GO:

Sign Up: Businesses can sign up online via the provided link: https://paylanes.sprocket.solutions/signup/merchant/cng

Submit KYC Documents: Comply with Know Your Customer regulations by submitting the necessary documents.

Access the Merchant Portal: Manage transactions and funds through a centralized dashboard.

OVERVIEW OF E-COMMERCE PAYMENT GATEWAYS IN THE BAHAMAS

Begin Transactions: Start making cash deposits and accepting card and digital payments.

Cash N' Go's Merchant Services extend beyond payment processing, with features like in-app advertising to enhance brand visibility and payroll services for easy salary disbursements. Integrated with Sand Dollar, their mobile wallet solution further solidifies their role in facilitating modern, digital financial transactions in The Bahamas.

CenPOS Payment

CenPOS is a trusted payment gateway provided by Elavon, designed to cater to the needs of major automotive, supply chain, heavy equipment, distribution, and manufacturing clients. It offers a comprehensive range of features, integrations, and flexible pricing options. Here's some information about CenPOS:

FEATURES:

- **All-in-one payment solutions:** CenPOS provides an end-to-end payment solution, which helps reduce costs and complexity and simplifies reporting and implementation processes.

- **Supply chain:** CenPOS offers authorization and settlement management features specifically designed for supply chain businesses, ensuring secure and efficient payment processing.

- **Automotive:** With CenPOS, auto dealerships can benefit from a secure payment experience tailored to their needs, enhancing customer satisfaction, and streamlining payment processes.

OVERVIEW OF E-COMMERCE PAYMENT GATEWAYS IN THE BAHAMAS

- **Heavy equipment:** CenPOS provides customized payment solutions for heavy equipment dealerships, facilitating seamless and secure transactions tailored to their unique requirements.

- **Wholesale distribution:** CenPOS streamlines payment processing for wholesale businesses, increasing visibility and efficiency throughout the payment lifecycle.

- **On-the-go payments:** CenPOS enables businesses to accept payments online through mobile devices, EMV card readers, or virtual terminals. It also offers digital billing and invoicing capabilities, allowing users to send invoices via email or text and receive payments through various methods.

PRICING:

Specific pricing details for CenPOS may vary depending on business size, transaction volume, and specific requirements. It is best to contact Elavon or the CenPOS sales team directly to get accurate pricing information tailored to your business needs.

INTEGRATION OPTIONS:

CenPOS integrates with industry-leading DMS (Dealer Management Systems) and ERP (Enterprise Resource Planning) systems, enabling businesses to leverage their existing infrastructure while benefiting from CenPOS's payment gateway functionality. This integration promotes a scalable payment infrastructure that is both simple and secure.

Security: CenPOS places a strong emphasis on data security. It implements rigorous measures such as encryption and tokenization to protect customers' credit card data, whether in use or at rest. This helps businesses meet compliance requirements and reduces the time spent on PCI DSS (Payment Card Industry Data Security Standard) compliance validation.

Simplicity and Flexibility: CenPOS offers tools to automate workflows, streamlining critical business operations. Users can create customized reports with the most valuable data, enabling them to gain insights and make informed decisions.

Charge Anywhere

Charge Anywhere is an exceptional e-commerce payment gateway that stands proudly among the diverse options available in The Bahamas. This innovative platform opens doors to secure online transactions, empowering merchants with various features tailored to their needs.

FEATURES:

Charge Anywhere offers a range of features that make it an attractive option for businesses. These features include:

- **Mobile payment functionality:** Charge Anywhere's solutions can enable mobile payments from various devices, including smartphones and tablets. This feature could include mobile wallet integration, QR code payments, or other contactless payment options.

- **Secure payment processing:** Charge Anywhere provides secure payment processing to enhance the safety and security of all transactions.

- **Fraud protection:** The platform uses advanced protection measures to prevent fraudulent transactions.

OVERVIEW OF E-COMMERCE PAYMENT GATEWAYS IN THE BAHAMAS

- **Multiple payment options:** Charge Anywhere supports multiple payment options, including credit cards, debit cards, and e-checks.

- **Cloud-based payment solutions:** Charge Anywhere's cloud-based platform allows for flexible and secure payment processing. This feature could include features like real-time reporting, fraud prevention tools, and automatic updates.
- **Integrated payment gateway solutions:** It integrates with various payment processors, allowing for streamlined payment processing across multiple channels.

- **Customization options:** The solutions it offers can be customized to fit the unique needs of individual businesses, from specific payment functionality to branding and user interface.

- **Compliance and certification:** Charge Anywhere is certified by major processors in the US and abroad, allowing for secure and compliant payment processing across a range of regulatory environments.

- **Retail POS solutions:** It offers a range of retail POS solutions that can integrate with existing systems or be deployed as standalone solutions. These solutions can offer features like inventory management, employee management, and loyalty program integration.

- **P2P encryption services:** Charge Anywhere offers encryption services to protect sensitive payment information during transmission, ensuring that customer data is always secure.

OVERVIEW OF E-COMMERCE PAYMENT GATEWAYS IN THE BAHAMAS

- **Open-platform technology:** Charge Anywhere's platform is hardware, processor, and operating-system neutral, allowing maximum flexibility in deploying payment solutions. This feature allows for easy integration with existing systems and enables the incorporation of new technologies as they emerge.

- **Support for large enterprises, developers, and independent sales organizations (ISOs):** Charge Anywhere's solutions are designed to meet the needs of businesses of all sizes and types, from independent developers to large enterprises. The platform can be tailored to fit the specific needs of individual businesses and can scale to accommodate growth.

PRICING:

Charge Anywhere provides tailor-made pricing options designed to meet each customer's unique requirements.

INTEGRATION OPTIONS:

Payment APIs: Charge Anywhere provides payment APIs (Application Programming Interfaces), allowing businesses to integrate payment processing with their websites or applications. With payment APIs, businesses can customize their payment pages, collect information, and process payments in real-time.

Virtual Terminals: Charge Anywhere also offers virtual terminals that allow businesses to process payments from any computer with an internet connection. Virtual terminals are particularly useful for businesses that process payments over the phone or via mail.

Mobile Payments: Charge Anywhere provides mobile payment options that allow businesses to accept payments on the go using their mobile devices. The mobile payment options include mobile POS (Point-of-Sale) systems, mobile card readers, and mobile payment apps.

E-commerce integrations: Charge Anywhere also integrates with various e-commerce platforms, such as [Magento](), [WooCommerce](), and [Shopify](). These integrations allow businesses to accept payments on their online stores through the Charge Anywhere payment gateway.

QuickBooks integration: It integrates with QuickBooks, an accounting software, to simplify business payment processing. With this integration, businesses can easily transfer transaction data from Charge Anywhere directly into QuickBooks, eliminating the need for manually entering the data.

CX Pay

CX Pay is a dynamic online payment platform that provides e-commerce businesses the flexibility and freedom to accept payments anytime, anywhere. Leveraging the latest compliance and fraud prevention technologies, CX Pay aims to create a safe, secure, and adaptable online payment environment designed to maximize customer satisfaction and revenue growth. Whether you're a start-up or an established enterprise, it aims to cater to your needs with its customizable solutions, which are suitable for handling transactions of any volume.

FEATURES:

The key features of CX Pay are engineered to provide a comprehensive and user-friendly payment solution. Here are the main features:

OVERVIEW OF E-COMMERCE PAYMENT GATEWAYS IN THE BAHAMAS

- **Comprehensive Payment Solution**: CX Pay offers various payment solutions, from basic setups to intricate systems, designed to meet diverse business requirements.

- **Advanced Fraud Prevention**: CX Pay's platform has top-tier security and fraud prevention measures to ensure safe and secure transactions.

- **High Volume Transaction Capability**: From small to large volumes, CX Pay can facilitate a high volume of transactions, offering scalability for your business.

- **Global Reach**: CX Pay has established itself as a trusted and flexible payment solutions provider and e-commerce application serving merchants worldwide.

- **Six Core Principles**: CX Pay operates on six core principles: Fairness, Passion, Innovation, Collaboration, Family, and Adventurousness. These principles reflect their commitment to providing excellent service, fostering strong relationships, and driving innovation.

PRICING:

CX Pay offers a comprehensive service pricing structure catering to merchants' different needs and requirements. Here is a breakdown of the pricing details:

1. **Signup/Start-up:** The initial start-up fee is US$ 175. This one-time payment covers the onboarding process and account setup.

OVERVIEW OF E-COMMERCE PAYMENT GATEWAYS IN THE BAHAMAS

2. **Wordpress/Woocommerce Integration:** For merchants using Wordpress/Woocommerce, CX Pay offers integration assistance for US$ 79. This fee is for the smooth integration of CX Pay's services with the merchant's website.

3. **Monthly Fee:** A monthly fee of US$ 15 provides access to CX Pay's payment processing services and ongoing support.

4. **Per Transaction Fee:** Each transaction processed through CX Pay costs US$ 0.35. There is no minimum monthly transaction requirement, allowing merchants flexibility in their transaction volumes.

5. **Commission on Incoming Monthly Fee:** CX Pay charges a commission of 0.25% on the incoming monthly fee for merchants with a transaction volume of up to $100,000 (USD). For merchants exceeding this volume, a new pricing structure may be applicable.

Additional Security Requirements:

For merchants working with CIBC Caribbean and Scotia, additional security measures are necessary. These include Payer Authentication (3DSecure) to promote secure transactions. The associated pricing for this extra security is as follows:

- **Setup:** US$ 25 (one-time fee)
- **Monthly:** US$ 10
- **Per Transaction:** US$ 0.10

On the other hand, merchants working with RBC require Extra Security/Risk Screening per Transaction (Decision Manager). The pricing for this extra security is as follows:

OVERVIEW OF E-COMMERCE PAYMENT GATEWAYS IN THE BAHAMAS

- **Setup:** US$ 25 (one-time fee)
- **Monthly:** US$ 10
- **Per Transaction:** US$ 0.15

Optional Extras:

CX Pay also offers additional services upon request. These extras enhance the merchant's payment processing capabilities and customer experience. The pricing for these optional extras is as follows:

- Tokenization: Tokenization allows clients to securely store their card details for future use, eliminating the need to re-enter them. The pricing for tokenization is as follows:
    - **Setup:** US$ 50 (one-time fee)
    - **Monthly:** US$ 10
    - **Per Transaction:** US$ 0.10

Please note that the pricing mentioned above does not include any fees or costs associated with your banking or financial institution. CX Pay assists merchants with the integration to Woocommerce, including testing, to facilitate a smooth transition before the account becomes active.

Overall, CX Pay provides a transparent pricing structure, allowing merchants to choose the services that suit their needs while maintaining flexibility in transaction volumes and additional security requirements.

OVERVIEW OF E-COMMERCE PAYMENT GATEWAYS IN THE BAHAMAS

INTEGRATION OPTIONS:

CX Pay provides a range of integrations with popular e-commerce and business platforms.

- **Wix, Shopify, WooCommerce, Magento**: These are e-commerce platforms. Integration means that CX Pay can be a payment gateway within these platforms, allowing customers to pay for products or services.

- **Brick Solutions, Zuora, Vindicia**: These are subscription and billing platforms. Integration with CX Pay enables these platforms to handle payments through CX Pay, providing seamless transactions for recurring payments or invoices.

It also provides the following integration solutions:

- **Decision Manager**: This is a fraud management solution typically offered by CyberSource. When integrated with CX Pay, it helps to evaluate and mitigate risks associated with online payments.

- **Payer Authentication 2.2 (3DSecure 2.2)**: This is a newer version of the 3DSecure protocol that provides additional security for online credit and debit card transactions. It allows the customer's bank to authenticate the transaction, reducing the likelihood of fraudulent payments.

- **Tokenization**: Integration with tokenization means that CX Pay converts sensitive data into non-sensitive equivalent tokens that have no exploitable value. This significantly enhances the security of online transactions.

By integrating these platforms and services, CX Pay can provide online businesses with a secure, efficient, and wide-ranging payment solution.

First Atlantic Commerce (FAC)

[First Atlantic Commerce (FAC)](#) **is a payment gateway for e-commerce in The Bahamas.**

FAC is a leading payment gateway utilized by numerous e-commerce companies across the Caribbean region. It offers a wide range of features, pricing plans, and integration options, making it a versatile solution for businesses of all sizes.

The FAC plugin, developed by **CSB Tech**, leverages the APIs provided by the payment gateway provider to deliver a robust payment processing and management solution.

Seamlessly integrating First Atlantic Commerce into their systems allows businesses to streamline their financial operations and offer customers a smooth and secure payment experience. With Atlantic Commerce, businesses can stay competitive by optimizing payment processes and driving customer satisfaction.

FEATURES:

FAC offers several features that make it an attractive option for businesses. These features include:

- **Merchant and Bank Options:** First Atlantic Commerce offers merchant and bank options for businesses, giving them flexibility in choosing the payment processing solution that best meets their needs.

OVERVIEW OF E-COMMERCE PAYMENT GATEWAYS IN THE BAHAMAS

- **Recurring billing:** FAC allows businesses to set up recurring billing for subscriptions and other services.

- **Multi-Currency Payment Processing:** First Atlantic Commerce offers online payment processing services that support transactions in multiple currencies, allowing businesses to accept payments from customers across the Caribbean, Bermuda, Central America, Canada, and the US.

- **PCI Certification:** First Atlantic Commerce is certified as compliant with the Payment Card Industry Data Security Standard (PCI DSS), which means that its payment processing platform meets stringent security standards to protect against payment card fraud.

- **Custom Payment Solutions:** First Atlantic Commerce offers custom payment solutions tailored to meet the specific needs of businesses in various industries, such as retail, e-commerce, travel, and hospitality.

- **Fraud Mitigation Solutions:** First Atlantic Commerce has powerful fraud mitigation solutions that help prevent fraudulent transactions and protect businesses from losses due to fraudulent activity.

- **Secure and Reliable Payments Platform:** First Atlantic Commerce has a secure and reliable payment processing platform. Their transactions are processed quickly and securely.

- **Excellent Customer Support:** First Atlantic Commerce provides amazing customer support to help businesses with

- **Award-Winning Technology Innovation:** First Atlantic Commerce has been recognized for its technology innovation in the online payment processing space.

PRICING:

First Atlantic Commerce offers competitively priced, custom payment solutions across the Caribbean, Bermuda, Central America, Canada, and the US.

The pricing for their payment processing services may vary depending on a range of factors, including the specific payment solutions and services a business requires, the volume of transactions processed, and the currencies supported.

INTEGRATION OPTIONS:

FAC integrates with various e-commerce platforms, including Shopify, WooCommerce, Magento, and OpenCart. The platform also provides businesses with a hosted payment page that can be easily integrated into their existing website.

Fygaro

With its roots firmly planted in cloud technology, Fygaro is revolutionizing the invoicing and billing industry by offering comprehensive payment gateway services. Catering to a broad spectrum of businesses, from start-ups to established entities, Fygaro provides various feature-rich solutions tailored to diverse business requirements and sizes.

OVERVIEW OF E-COMMERCE PAYMENT GATEWAYS IN THE BAHAMAS

Regarded as a big player for contemporary commerce, it provides a smooth, secure, and effective payment processing experience, establishing it as the preferred option for businesses in The Bahamas.

How does Fygaro work?

Fygaro works by providing businesses with a cloud-based invoicing and billing platform that integrates with a payment gateway to facilitate secure online payments.

Here's how it works:

Create an account: Businesses sign up for a Fygaro account and provide basic information about their business.

Customize invoices: Fygaro allows businesses to customize their invoices with their branding and logo. They can also add products or services they offer and set up recurring invoices for regular customers.

Send invoices: Once they are set up, businesses can send them to their customers via email, text, or print.

Payment collection: Fygaro's payment gateway lets customers securely pay their invoices online using credit cards, debit cards, or bank transfers. Fygaro supports a variety of payment methods, including Visa, Mastercard, American Express, Discover, and more.

Track payments: Fygaro also provides businesses with tools to track their payments and generate reports, making it easier to manage their finances and reconcile payments.

OVERVIEW OF E-COMMERCE PAYMENT GATEWAYS IN THE BAHAMAS

Fygaro simplifies the invoicing and payment process for businesses, allowing them to focus on growing their business rather than spending time on administrative tasks.

FEATURES:

Fygaro provides a range of features that make it a compelling choice for businesses. These features include:

- **Multi-currency support:** Fygaro supports multiple currencies, making it easy for businesses to accept customer payments in different countries.

- **Customizable payment pages:** Businesses can customize their payment pages to match their brand and provide a seamless payment experience for their customers.

- **Recurring payments:** Fygaro allows businesses to set up recurring payments for subscriptions and other recurring charges.

- **Multiple payment options:** Fygaro supports multiple payment options, including credit cards, debit cards, and PayPal.

- **Invoice management:** The platform offers features that allow businesses to create and manage invoices, track payments, and send payment reminders.

PRICING:

Fygaro offers several pricing plans that cater to businesses of varied sizes and needs.

OVERVIEW OF E-COMMERCE PAYMENT GATEWAYS IN THE BAHAMAS

It offers three different payment options: Basic, Pro, and Advanced. Each option has its own features to suit different business needs.

Basic Payment Option:

The basic payment option allows unlimited products and one user access to the Fygaro account. It includes the Fygaro Shop, which provides tools to build a custom web store. This option also includes payment buttons for social media, chats, invoices, and more. It offers gateway integrations to accept credit and debit card payments, manual order creation, basic reports, support, multiple inventories, discount codes, and currency conversion.

Pro Payment Option:

The Pro payment option is designed for businesses with more extensive needs. It includes all the features of the basic payment option plus some additional benefits. This option allows up to five users to access the Fygaro account. It offers Payment Button Integration with Hooks, allowing more customization options. This option also includes integrations to automatically quote and get labels from providers like DHL.

Advanced Payment Option:

The advanced payment option is the most comprehensive of the three options. It includes all the features of the Pro payment option, plus some additional benefits. This option allows up to ten users to access the Fygaro account.

It offers the same Payment Button Integration with Hooks as the Pro option. This option also includes creating custom reports and access to more extensive support.

OVERVIEW OF E-COMMERCE PAYMENT GATEWAYS IN THE BAHAMAS

INTEGRATION OPTIONS:

Fygaro integrates with various e-commerce platforms, including Shopify, WooCommerce, and Magento. The platform also provides businesses with a payment API that can be integrated into their existing website or mobile app.

Its pricing plans and integration options make it a flexible solution for businesses of all sizes.

Kanoo

Kanoo is another e-commerce payment gateway available in The Bahamas. It is a payment processing platform that offers businesses an easy way to accept payments online. It is a secure and reliable payment gateway trusted by many businesses nationwide.

Kanoo offers its own plugin for WooCommerce, resulting in CSB Tech discontinuing the sale of theirs. Additionally, by leveraging their API to create custom solutions for web and mobile applications, businesses can enhance their financial operations and provide customers with a secure and hassle-free payment experience. Their API offers a range of features and benefits that can help businesses optimize their payment processes and stay ahead in today's competitive landscape.

FEATURES:

Kanoo offers a variety of features that make it an attractive option for businesses. These features include:

- **Secure payment processing:** Kanoo offers secure payment processing that promotes overall safe and secure transactions.

OVERVIEW OF E-COMMERCE PAYMENT GATEWAYS IN THE BAHAMAS

- **Licensed by the Central Bank of The Bahamas:** Kanoo is licensed by the Central Bank of The Bahamas as a Non-Bank Electronic Retail Payment Institution, which adds credibility to the platform.

- **Point-of-sale system for digital payments:** Kanoo offers a state-of-the-art point-of-sale system allowing businesses to accept digital payments for less than commercial banks charge. This functionality accelerates transaction processing, enabling businesses to manage transactions at a pace that matches the rapidity of everyday life.

- **Audience Relationship Manager (ARM):** Kanoo's ARM is a powerful marketing tool that helps businesses manage all their marketing needs from a single portal. This feature empowers merchants to create marketing campaigns, manage audience analytics, incentivize, monetize, and connect with existing and future customers. The ARM boosts brand recognition, stimulates sales growth, and fortifies customer allegiance.

- **Campaign Building and Sales Boosting:** Kanoo allows businesses to build and execute different types of campaigns, such as Awareness, Sales, and Loyalty Campaigns. Awareness campaigns help businesses strengthen brand awareness by encouraging consumers to trade cards with them and share their business with others in exchange for incentives. Sales campaigns encourage consumers to shop with the business by giving them incentives. Loyalty campaigns boost customer loyalty by offering rewards for regular digital purchases.

- **Data Analytics:** Kanoo helps businesses analyze and optimize engagement and revenue data to strategically position their brand in front of their target audience. Companies can leverage analytics, digital rewards, promotional activities, and campaigns to enhance customer involvement, maintain customer loyalty, and increase revenue.

- **Customer Relationship Management:** Kanoo helps businesses bridge the gap between them and their customers by understanding and anticipating their needs before they ask. This feature is essential for businesses looking to enhance customer satisfaction and long-term revenue.

- **Connectivity:** Kanoo's app allows users to connect with their family, friends, colleagues, and businesses, making it easier for them to stay in touch and connected.

PRICING:

Kanoo offers three different pricing plans: Gold, Platinum, and Diamond. Each plan comes with different features and pricing, depending on your needs as a merchant.

1. Gold Plan

The Gold Plan is Kanoo's most basic pricing plan. It comes with a free monthly subscription and a merchant processing fee of 2.5% per transaction. This plan is ideal for small businesses that want to start using Kanoo's services without committing to a monthly fee.

- **Brand Awareness Campaigns**

    If you choose the Gold Plan, you can still use Kanoo's Brand Awareness Campaigns. These include promotions that help you get the word out about your business. The cost of these promotions is $13.20.

- **Loyalty Campaigns**

    Unfortunately, the Gold Plan does not include any loyalty campaigns. This means you won't have access to punch cards or other loyalty rewards programs.

- **Sales Campaigns**

    The Gold Plan also does not include any sales campaigns. You won't be able to create rewards coupons or offer coupon redemption with this plan.

- **Connect & Others**

    Finally, the Gold Plan does not include any of Kanoo's other features. This includes the Connect Zone, Kanoo POS App, and Data Analytics. You won't have access to products, business locations, or payment gateway integration.

2. Platinum Plan

The Platinum Plan is Kanoo's mid-tier pricing plan. It comes with a monthly subscription fee of $11.00 and a merchant processing fee of 2.5% per transaction.

- **Brand Awareness Campaigns**

    You can still access Kanoo's brand awareness campaigns with the Platinum Plan. The cost of these promotions is also $11.00.

- **Loyalty Campaigns**

  Unlike the Gold Plan, the Platinum Plan includes access to punch cards. This means you can set up loyalty rewards programs for your customers.

- **Sales Campaigns**

  The Platinum Plan also includes creating rewards coupons and offering coupon redemption. The cost of rewards coupons is $1.10 per day.

- **Connect & Others**

  The Platinum Plan includes access to the Connect Zone, Kanoo POS App, and Data Analytics. However, you won't have access to products, business locations, or payment gateway integration.

3. Diamond Plan

The Diamond Plan is Kanoo's most advanced pricing plan. It comes with a monthly subscription fee of $41.98 and a merchant processing fee of 2.5% per transaction.

- **Brand Awareness Campaigns**

  The Diamond Plan includes access to Kanoo's Brand Awareness Campaigns. The cost of promotions is $8.80.

- **Loyalty Campaigns**

  The Diamond Plan includes access to punch cards, like the Platinum Plan.

- **Sales Campaigns**

The Diamond Plan also includes Rewards Coupons and Coupon Redemption at no additional cost. This allows you to create and offer coupons to your customers, which can help drive sales.

- **Connect & Others**

    The Diamond Plan includes all of Kanoo's other features, including the Connect Zone, Kanoo POS App, and Data Analytics. This plan allows you to access products, business locations, and payment gateway integration.

Mastercard Payment Gateway Services

Mastercard Payment Gateway Services is a payment processing solution suite that enables businesses to accept online payments. It is a versatile payment gateway offering various payment options, including credit and debit card payments, e-wallets, and bank transfers.

FEATURES:

- **Multiple Payment Options:** Mastercard Payment Gateway Services offers a range of payment options to customers, including credit and debit cards, e-wallets, and bank transfers.

- **Fraud Protection:** The payment gateway offers advanced fraud detection and prevention features to protect businesses and customers from fraudulent activities.

- **Multi-Currency Support:** Mastercard Payment Gateway Services supports multiple currencies, making it easy for

OVERVIEW OF E-COMMERCE PAYMENT GATEWAYS IN THE BAHAMAS

businesses to accept customer payments in different countries.

- **Easy Integration:** Mastercard Payment Gateway Services can be easily integrated into most e-commerce platforms and websites with the help of APIs and plugins.

- **Customer Management:** The payment gateway also offers customer management tools, such as account creation, order tracking, and payment history.

PRICING:

As a Mastercard merchant, you pay your acquirer a Merchant Discount Rate (MDR) for card acceptance services, including interchange fees paid by acquirers to card issuers.

Mastercard sets the interchange rates, a delicate balance between benefits to cardholders and merchants. Different interchange rates for different merchant categories, transaction types, and criteria must be met to qualify for a particular rate.

Rates are updated semiannually and can be found on the Mastercard website. Still, it's best to speak with your acquirer if you have questions about Mastercard interchange rates or card acceptance agreements.

INTEGRATION OPTIONS:

Hosted Payment Page: Mastercard Payment Gateway Services offers a hosted payment page solution that enables businesses to accept payments online without needing a website or e-commerce platform. This option provides a simple and quick way to start accepting payments.

OVERVIEW OF E-COMMERCE PAYMENT GATEWAYS IN THE BAHAMAS

Hosted Checkout: It also offers a hosted checkout solution that enables businesses to accept payments on their website. This option provides a secure and easy-to-use payment interface for customers.

API Integration: For businesses that want more control over the payment process, Mastercard Payment Gateway Services provides API resources enabling developers to integrate the payment gateway into their systems. This option provides greater flexibility and customization options.

Shopping Cart Plugins: Mastercard Payment Gateway Services has developed plugins for popular e-commerce platforms such as WooCommerce, Magento, and Shopify. These plugins enable businesses to easily integrate the payment gateway into their online store.

Mobile Integration: Mastercard Payment Gateway Services provides mobile payment integration options, allowing businesses to accept payments on the go through mobile devices. This option provides flexibility for businesses with mobile payment needs.

Virtual Terminal: For businesses that accept payments over the phone, Mastercard Payment Gateway Services provides a virtual terminal solution that enables businesses to process payments manually. This option provides flexibility for businesses with diverse payment channels.

Payoneer

Payoneer is a popular payment gateway that enables businesses in The Bahamas to receive payments from customers worldwide. It offers a range of payment solutions, including cross-border payments, mass payouts, and online payments.

OVERVIEW OF E-COMMERCE PAYMENT GATEWAYS IN THE BAHAMAS

FEATURES:

- **Payment Solution for eCommerce Businesses:** Payoneer provides a simple and comprehensive payment solution, particularly for online sellers.

- **International Payments:** Millions of online sellers choose Payoneer's eCommerce payment solutions to help grow their business internationally. Payoneer enables sellers to receive global payments as easily as local payments.

- **Top eCommerce Marketplaces:** Sellers on global marketplaces such as Amazon and Wish can make money and get paid with Payoneer's easy global payment method.

- **Multiple Currencies:** Payoneer enables sellers to reach more customers in the U.S., Europe, the U.K., and more with accounts in multiple currencies.

- **Free In-Network Payments:** Payoneer lets sellers pay their suppliers and contractors for free with fast in-network payments.

- **Local Bank Account Withdrawal:** Sellers can easily withdraw their funds to a local bank account.

- **Payment Tracking:** Payoneer enables sellers to track upcoming payments and view their payment history for their eCommerce stores.

- **Recurring Payments:** Sellers may allow vendors that require recurring payments to debit their accounts automatically.

OVERVIEW OF E-COMMERCE PAYMENT GATEWAYS IN THE BAHAMAS

- **Global Receiving Accounts:** Payoneer offers customers receiving accounts for local transfers in EUR, USD, and GBP. Sellers can accept payments directly in more currencies with Payoneer's global receiving accounts.

- **Manage Currencies:** Payoneer enables sellers to easily manage currencies and transfer between different Payoneer currency balances to pay their suppliers and service providers in their preferred currency.

- **Immediate In-Network Payments:** Payoneer makes it easy to pay in-network suppliers for free with fast and secure payments received in up to 2 hours.

- **Amazon Store Manager:** The Amazon Store Manager helps business owners see the "big picture" by aggregating all Amazon income information in one place, making it simple to track which stores generate the most revenue.

- **Customizable View:** Sellers can customize their view by filtering by transaction type, status, and printing or exporting the table for their records in Excel or PDF format. They can also generate a monthly activity statement with a button.

- **Customizable View:** Sellers can customize their view by filtering by transaction type, status, and printing or exporting the table for their records in Excel or PDF format. They can also generate a monthly activity statement with a button.

- Acceptance of a wide range of payment methods, including credit and debit cards, e-checks, and digital wallets.

OVERVIEW OF E-COMMERCE PAYMENT GATEWAYS IN THE BAHAMAS

- Advanced fraud detection and prevention tools.

- Access to detailed reporting and transaction history.

- Recurring billing options for subscription-based businesses.

PRICING:

Payoneer offers competitive pricing with transparent fees. The pricing plans are as follows:

Credit card transactions (all currencies): 3%

If you receive payment via credit card through Payoneer, a fee of 3% will be deducted from the total amount received. This fee is applicable for transactions made in any currency.

ACH bank debit transactions: 1%

If you receive payment via ACH bank debit through Payoneer, a fee of 1% will be deducted from the total amount received.

Receiving payments from other Payoneer users: 0%

If you receive payment from another Payoneer user, no fees are involved.

Transferring funds from Payoneer to your bank account: $1.50 (local currency); 2% (non-local currency)

A flat fee of $1.50 applies when you send money from your Payoneer account to a bank account in the same currency. However, for transfers to a bank account in a different currency, a 2% fee is levied.

Batch payments to up to 200 bank accounts: 2%

OVERVIEW OF E-COMMERCE PAYMENT GATEWAYS IN THE BAHAMAS

You can use Payoneer's batch payment service if you need to simultaneously make multiple payments to up to 200 bank accounts. However, a fee of 2% will be charged for this service.

Sending payments from your Payoneer account: 0% to 2%

If you need to send payments from your Payoneer account to other users or vendors, the fees will depend on the payment method and the currency used. For instance, if you send a payment in the same currency as your account balance, the fee will be 0%. However, if you send a payment in a different currency, the fee can increase to 2%.

Currency conversion fees: 3.5% (Payoneer MasterCard); 0.5% (between Payoneer accounts)

If you use Payoneer's MasterCard to make a payment in a currency different from your account balance, a fee of 3.5% will be charged for the currency conversion. However, if you transfer funds between Payoneer accounts in different currencies, the fee is only 0.5%.

There is no monthly fee, however, there is a $29.95 fee for every 12 months of inactivity.

Payoneer does not charge a monthly fee for its services. However, if you haven't used your account for 12 months or more, a fee of $29.95 will be charged as an inactivity fee.

INTEGRATION OPTIONS:

Payoneer's integration capabilities are as varied as the needs of its users, with a range of options catering to popular **e-commerce platforms** like Shopify, WooCommerce, and Magento, as well as **API integration** for those who require custom-built solutions.

OVERVIEW OF E-COMMERCE PAYMENT GATEWAYS IN THE BAHAMAS

Plug n Pay

Plug n Pay is a popular payment gateway many online businesses in the country use.

Plug n Pay works by providing cloud-based payment processing software that enables organizations to manage their payment processes on a centralized platform. It uses the WebXpress Processing Gateway to process credit card transactions, calculate sales tax, and add e-commerce capabilities to a website.

When a customer makes a purchase, the payment information is securely processed through Plug n Pay's software, which administrators can access through a dashboard. The software then sends customizable confirmation emails to customers about their purchases, shipping information, special offers, or support.

In addition, Plug n Pay allows organizations to track sales activities in real-time, configure access permissions for employees, and send invoices to customers for payment. It also helps businesses block risky transactions from questionable I.P. addresses and credit card numbers and facilitates integration with various third-party accounting systems, including QuickBooks.

It offers a wide range of features, pricing plans, and integration options, making it a flexible solution for businesses of all sizes.

FEATURES:

Plug-n-Pay offers a variety of features that make it an attractive option for businesses. These features include:

OVERVIEW OF E-COMMERCE PAYMENT GATEWAYS IN THE BAHAMAS

- **Fraud protection:** The platform uses advanced fraud protection measures to prevent fraudulent transactions.

- **Multiple payment options:** Plug n Pay supports multiple payment options, including credit cards, debit cards, and e-checks.

- **Customizable checkout:** Businesses can customize the checkout process to fit their brand and customer needs.

- **Reporting and analytics:** Plug n Pay allows businesses to access detailed reports and analytics on their transactions to track sales and revenue.

- **Centralized platform:** With Plug n Pay, organizations can manage all their payment processes in one place, making tracking sales activities and accessing data easier.

- **Customizable confirmation emails:** Plug n Pay's software sends customizable confirmation emails to customers about their purchases, shipping information, special offers, or support, which helps to build customer loyalty.

- **Integration with accounting systems:** Plug n Pay can be integrated with various third-party accounting systems, including QuickBooks, which makes it easier for organizations to manage their financial records.

- **Risky transaction blocking:** Plug n Pay helps businesses block risky transactions from questionable IP addresses and credit card numbers, which helps prevent fraud.

- **Self-service interface:** Clients can use the self-service interface to access passwords, renew expired subscriptions, edit account details, and cancel memberships according to requirements, which provides convenience and flexibility.

PRICING:

Plug n Pay offers a zero-cost credit card processing solution for businesses, where they can sell for $100 and receive $100 for credit card transactions. The pricing plan is simple and transparent, with the option to pay only for debit card transactions at a low cost.

Plug n Pay's turnkey solution complies with all rules and regulations, and there are no PCI exposures for in-office or in-person transactions.

Customers can choose between credit and debit cards, and for credit cards, they can opt to pay the fee. Different pricing plans exist for different sectors, such as business surcharging and intelligent rates for Government and Education, where the pricing is fair and transparent.

INTEGRATION OPTIONS:

Plug n Pay integrates with various e-commerce platforms, including WooCommerce, Shopify, Magento, PrestaShop, Foxy, 1ShoppingCart, and OpenCart.

The platform also provides businesses with a hosted payment page that can be easily integrated into their existing website.

Plug n Pay offers a wide range of features, pricing plans, and integration options, making it a flexible solution for businesses of all sizes. With secure payment processing, advanced fraud protection, and customizable checkout options, Plug n Pay is a popular e-commerce payment gateway in The Bahamas.

OVERVIEW OF E-COMMERCE PAYMENT GATEWAYS IN THE BAHAMAS

Sand Dollar

The Sand Dollar is a Central Bank Digital Currency (CBDC) issued by the Central Bank of The Bahamas, representing a digital form of the Bahamian dollar (B$). It's not a typical payment gateway but a government-backed digital currency designed to improve financial transaction efficiency and inclusivity in The Bahamas.

While distinct from conventional e-commerce payment systems, the Sand Dollar seamlessly integrates with local e-wallet solutions, offering businesses a reliable and secure digital transaction option.

This initiative marks a significant step in modernizing the Bahamian financial landscape, particularly benefiting those with limited access to traditional banking.

FEATURES:

- **Seamless Integration:** Sand Dollar can be integrated into various payment systems, making it an interoperable option for businesses.

- **Resilient Transactions:** It boasts offline functionality, allowing transactions to proceed without constant internet connectivity.

- **Instant Processing:** The gateway provides near-instantaneous transaction validation for real-time processing.

- **Enhanced Business Support:** Sand Dollar is equipped to support businesses with tailored fintech solutions and POS terminal compatibility.

- **Compliance and Security:** It maintains a fully auditable trail of transactions while ensuring user confidentiality within a strict regulatory framework.

- **Exclusive Domestic Use:** Sand Dollar emphasizes its use for domestic transactions, aligning with the country's regulatory policies.

- **Multi-Layered Security:** Users benefit from multi-factor authentication protocols to authorize transactions securely.

- **Digital Identity Verification:** The service integrates digital ID solutions, bolstering the security and reliability of transactions.

PRICING:

Merchant-Focused Financial Structuring: While specific pricing is not mentioned, merchant wallets suggest a scalable system with holding limits appropriate for a range of business operations.

Unlimited Transactions: The gateway allows unlimited transactions within the holding limit, providing flexibility for business operations.

INTEGRATION OPTIONS:

Business Enrollment: Companies looking to utilize the Sand Dollar must go through an enrollment process with the Central Bank's authorized financial institutions (AFIs).

Documentation for Enrollment: A valid business license and VAT certificate are prerequisites for businesses to integrate Sand Dollar.

Customizable Wallet Options: Depending on the AFI chosen, businesses can select an e-wallet that best suits their needs, highlighting the customizable nature of Sand Dollar.

OVERVIEW OF E-COMMERCE PAYMENT GATEWAYS IN THE BAHAMAS

The Sand Dollar stands out as a distinct digital currency platform in The Bahamas, specifically designed to meet the needs of its users with its forward-thinking features and robust security measures. For businesses operating within this beautiful archipelago, it represents a secure, efficient, and modern approach to processing transactions.

SunCash

SunCash is a popular payment gateway platform in The Bahamas that offers a range of services for e-commerce businesses. As a payment gateway, SunCash facilitates online transactions between customers and merchants, allowing businesses to accept payments from customers using their mobile devices.

The [SunCash plugin](), a product developed by **CSB Tech**, is an advanced payment processing and management solution that aims to streamline financial operations for businesses.

The SunCash plugin empowers businesses to provide customers with a seamless and highly secure payment experience by seamlessly integrating with multiple payment gateway providers.

By leveraging the robust APIs these payment gateway providers offer, the SunCash plugin equips businesses with the tools to optimize their payment processes and enhance overall customer satisfaction.

FEATURES:

SunCash offers a variety of features that make it an attractive option for e-commerce businesses. Some of its key features include:

- **Mobile Payments:** SunCash allows customers to make payments using their mobile devices, making it a convenient option for shoppers who prefer to purchase on the go.

OVERVIEW OF E-COMMERCE PAYMENT GATEWAYS IN THE BAHAMAS

- **Mobile Payment Solution:** SunCash is a mobile payment solution that enables customers to make payments securely using their mobile phones.

- **Low Discount Rates:** SunCash offers the lowest discount rates in the market, which makes it an attractive option for customers.

- **Bill Pay and Mobile Top-up:** In addition to accepting payments, SunCash also provides bill pay and mobile top-up services.

- **Integration with Existing POS Systems:** SunCash can be seamlessly integrated with a merchant's existing point-of-sale (POS) system, making it easy for them to accept SunCash payments.

- **Lower Discount Rates and Cash Handling Costs for Merchants:** Merchants using SunCash can benefit from lower discount rates and cash handling costs.

- **Multiple Payment Options:** SunCash supports payment options such as QRCode, BarCode, Manual Code, tap to Pay, and PIN.

- **Receipts:** After processing a transaction, merchants can print, email, or SMS POS receipts to the customer.

- **Secure Transactions:** SunCash offers secure payment processing, thus their transactions are safe and secure. It uses encryption technology to protect users' data and transactions, and its servers are housed in a secure data center.

- **Customer Support:** SunCash provides business customer support through its website and in-person at SunCash locations.

PRICING:

SunCash takes security seriously and employs various measures to protect users' funds and personal information.

Its PCI-compliant payment processing uses encryption technology to secure all transactions and user data. SunCash also regularly monitors its systems for potential security threats and takes action to mitigate any risks.

SunCash is a robust payment gateway platform that offers a range of features and integration options for e-commerce businesses.

Its transparent pricing and commitment to security make it a trusted and reliable option for businesses looking to accept mobile payments and expand their global reach.

Regarding transaction fees, SunCash applies a 1% fee to all transactions, coupled with a fixed fee of $0.20. Moreover, there is a 4% convenience fee on transactions. Merchants have the option to either absorb this fee or pass it on to the customer.

For an enhanced customer experience, it is recommended that merchants absorb the convenience fee. This approach can foster goodwill and increase customer loyalty by minimizing the additional costs they incur.

OVERVIEW OF E-COMMERCE PAYMENT GATEWAYS IN THE BAHAMAS

INTEGRATION OPTIONS:

SunCash can be integrated with various e-commerce platforms, including Shopify, WooCommerce, Magento, and more. SunCash's integration options make it a convenient and hassle-free payment gateway solution for e-commerce businesses.

Tilopay

Tilopay is an e-commerce payment gateway that provides businesses a quick, easy, and secure way to accept online payments.

With Tilopay, businesses can accept credit card payments from customers worldwide, settling everything in their local currency.

List of Pre-Integrated Banks

Tilopay is pre-integrated with several banks, making it easier for businesses to process payments. The banks include **Scotiabank**, **RBC**, and **CIBC**.

Accepted Payment Methods

Tilopay accepts payments through credit cards such as **Visa, Mastercard, and American Express.** The commission charged for transactions is 1%, which is affordable for businesses of all sizes.

Features:

Tilopay is a payment gateway designed to facilitate digital transactions for businesses of all sizes. It offers a range of solutions and functionalities that help businesses process payments easily and securely. Here are some of the key features of Tilopay:

- **Access to all Solutions and Functionalities**

By registering with Tilopay, businesses can access a comprehensive suite of payment solutions and functionalities. This includes Tilopay Link, Tilopay Checkout, and Tilopay Repeat. Tilopay Link allows businesses to generate payment links that can be shared with customers via email or social media. At the same time, Tilopay Checkout enables businesses to integrate payment options into their websites. Tilopay Repeat allows businesses to set up recurring payments for subscriptions and other services.

- **International Payments**

With Tilopay, businesses can charge customers worldwide and settle payments in their local currency. This feature is particularly useful for businesses that operate globally and need to accept payments from customers in different countries. Tilopay enables businesses to expand their customer base and increase revenue by facilitating international payments.

- **Secure Payments**

Tilopay takes security seriously and provides businesses with digital security and anti-fraud measures, including 3DS 2.0. Thus, Tilopay's transactions are secure and protected from fraudulent activities. Additionally, they comply with data security standards, including PCI, to protect customer data.

- **Administrative Panel**

Tilopay offers an easy-to-use administrative panel that allows businesses to view their earnings, transactions, and settlements in real time. This feature enables businesses to keep track of their financials easily, monitor payment activity, and reconcile payments quickly.

- **Tilopay API and SDK**

    Tilopay offers an API and SDK that businesses can use to build a personalized customer checkout experience. The integration provides the functionality to use the security provided by Tilopay in the payment form. The configuration process of this integration requires basic or intermediate knowledge of JavaScript and HTML technologies.

PRICING

Tilopay is a cutting-edge payment processing platform that offers a simple and cost-effective solution for businesses of all sizes. With its innovative pricing model, Tilopay has quickly gained popularity among businesses looking for a reliable payment processing partner that doesn't break the bank.

Affordability is the key feature of Tilopay's pricing model. The platform charges a commission of only 1% for all transactions, making it an attractive option for small and large businesses.

This commission is significantly lower than most traditional payment processors charge and doesn't come with hidden fees or additional costs.

One of the most significant advantages of Tilopay's pricing model is that no fixed costs or monthly payments are required to use the platform. This means businesses can process as many transactions as they want without worrying about extra costs. This is particularly beneficial for small businesses with limited cash flow and need to keep their expenses low.

HONORABLE MENTIONS

Vital Entities in The Bahamas' Digital Payment Ecosystem

The digital economy of The Bahamas is advancing through the collaboration of financial intermediaries like:

- Clearing Banks
- Credit Unions
- Money Transmission Businesses (MTBs) and
- Payment Service Providers (PSPs)

These players are key to enriching the e-commerce and digital payment sectors and building a financial system that is more inclusive and streamlined.

MTBs and PSPs pioneered mobile wallets, something banks and credit unions weren't expected to do at the start of digital currency. Now, all financial entities contribute by connecting deposit accounts to mobile wallets, improving customer checks, and making foreign exchange transactions easier.

The Central Bank also promotes a united financial system by encouraging PSPs to use current Know-Your-Customer (KYC) documents.

Financial institutions are also asked to share KYC confirmations for digital currency transactions. This aims to simplify digital dealings and promote safe, instant transactions, contributing to a modernized financial setup in The Bahamas.

Omni

Omni, The Bahamas' largest remittance company, operates nine locations with over sixty employees. It offers diverse remittance options through CAM, JMMB, MoneyGram, UNI Transfers, mobile top-ups, and bill payments. Omni's twelve-year growth showcases its commitment to revolutionizing financial services and expanding offerings.

MobileAssist™

MobileAssist™ offers a free app that simplifies access to commercial, governmental, and non-profit organizations. It provides directions, notifications, coupons, and a unified communication platform, enhancing user convenience and accessibility.

Island Pay

Island Pay introduces large-scale payment solutions focusing on underserved areas as the first licensed Payment Service Provider and Electronic Money Institution by the Central Bank of The Bahamas. It offers 24/7 wallet access, supporting financial transactions for the 'underbanked' and 'unbanked,' and transforms cash-based tasks into efficient digital transactions.

MoneyMaxx

MoneyMaxx, with over 20 locations and 100 staff, delivers time-saving financial solutions through face-to-face and mobile wallet services. It facilitates bill payments, gift card purchases, and money transfers, emphasizing convenience and efficiency.

HONORABLE MENTIONS

These entities—Omni, MobileAssist™, Island Pay, and MoneyMaxx—are big players in advancing The Bahamas' financial inclusion and digital readiness. Their innovative services support the Sand Dollar initiative and future digital payment advancements.

As The Bahamas' digital economy grows, their contributions will be crucial in creating a more connected and financially inclusive society. Their efforts promise a future of accessible, efficient, and secure financial transactions for all Bahamians.

BANKING INTEGRATIONS IN THE BAHAMAS

Banking Integrations in The Bahamas

Banks in The Bahamas have implemented direct integration and e-wallet gateways to streamline financial transactions. In this segment, we will explore these gateways employed by different banks, highlighting their integration partners and capabilities.

Direct Integration Gateways:

1. **Plug n Pay: Integration Partners – Canadian Imperial Bank of Commerce (CIBC), Royal Bank of Canada (RBC).**

    This gateway allows CIBC and RBC customers in The Bahamas to accept payments securely and efficiently.

BANKING INTEGRATIONS IN THE BAHAMAS

2. **First Atlantic Commerce: Integration Partners - CIBC, Scotiabank, RBC.**

   Businesses using this gateway can accept online payments, manage risk, and conduct transactions seamlessly with CIBC, Scotiabank, and RBC customers.

3. **Charge Anywhere: Integration Partner - Fidelity Bank.**

   This gateway enables Fidelity Bank customers to accept payments through various channels, including mobile devices, point-of-sale terminals, and e-commerce platforms.

4. **Fygaro: Integration Partners - CIBC, RBC, Scotiabank.**

   Fygaro provides direct integration gateways for CIBC, RBC, and Scotiabank customers. Businesses can automate invoicing, manage inventory, and accept payments online efficiently.

5. **CX Pay: Integration Partners - CIBC, RBC, Scotiabank.**

   CX Pay offers direct integration gateways for CIBC, RBC, and Scotiabank customers. Businesses can accept payments in multiple currencies, manage subscriptions, and mitigate fraud risks.

6. **CenPos: Integration Partner - Bank of The Bahamas (BOM).**

   CenPos provides a direct integration gateway for Bank of The Bahamas customers. Businesses can accept payments securely, manage customer data, and streamline financial operations.

7. **Tilopay: Integration Partners - CIBC, Scotiabank, RBC.**

   Tilopay offers direct integration gateways for CIBC, Scotiabank, and RBC customers. Their platform facilitates online payments, invoicing, and business management, enhancing financial efficiency.

E-wallet Gateways:

1. **Kanoo: Integration Partners - CIBC, Scotiabank, RBC, Fidelity, Bank of The Bahamas (BOB), Commonwealth Bank (CB).**

   Kanoo provides an e-wallet gateway integrated with multiple banks in The Bahamas. Users can make secure payments, transfer funds, and manage transactions conveniently through a digital wallet.

2. **SunCash: Integration Partners - CIBC, Scotiabank, RBC, Fidelity, Bank of The Bahamas (BOB), Commonwealth Bank (CB).**

   SunCash offers an e-wallet gateway that enables users to conduct financial transactions, including payments and transfers, through partnered banks in The Bahamas. The solution promotes convenience and accessibility.

3. **Payoneer: Integration Partners - CIBC, Scotiabank, RBC, Fidelity, Bank of The Bahamas (BOB), Commonwealth Bank (CB).**

   Payoneer offers a global e-wallet solution, efficiently facilitating cross-border payments and currency conversion. Integrated with leading Bahamian banks, it supports seamless transactions for individuals and businesses, enhancing financial operations internationally.

4. **Cash N' Go: Integration Partners - CIBC, Scotiabank, RBC, Fidelity, Bank of The Bahamas (BOB), Commonwealth Bank (CB).**

   Cash N' Go provides a user-friendly e-wallet service, enabling quick mobile top-ups, bill payments, and transfers. Its integration with major Bahamian banks ensures convenient access to financial services, streamlining daily transactions.

PAYMENT GATEWAY REFERENCE GUIDE: Direct & E-Wallet Bank Integration

DIRECT INTEGRATION GATEWAYS

Banks	Plug n' Pay	First Atlantic Commerce	Charge Anywhere	Fygaro	CX Pay	CenPOS	Tilopay
CIBC Caribbean (CIBC)	✖	✖		✖	✖		✖
Scotiabank		✖		✖	✖		✖
Royal Bank of Canada (RBC)	✖	✖		✖	✖		✖
Fidelity			✖				
Commonwealth Bank (CB)							
Bank of The Bahamas (BOB)						✖	

E-WALLET GATEWAYS

Banks	Kanoo	Suncash	Payoneer	Cash N Go
CIBC Caribbean (CIBC)	✖	✖	✖	✖
Scotiabank	✖	✖	✖	✖
Royal Bank of Canada (RBC)	✖	✖	✖	✖
Fidelity	✖	✖	✖	✖
Commonwealth Bank (CB)	✖	✖	✖	✖
Bank of The Bahamas (BOB)	✖	✖	✖	✖

CONCLUSIONS

In conclusion, e-commerce is a growing industry in The Bahamas, allowing businesses to reach a wider audience and expand their customer base beyond physical storefronts. This guide has explored the various e-commerce options available in The Bahamas, including hosted e-commerce platforms, custom e-commerce websites, and mobile commerce.

We have discussed the advantages and disadvantages of each option, as well as best practices for setting up an online store. Additionally, we have reviewed the **various e-commerce payment gateways available in The Bahamas**, including Plug n Pay, Fygaro, First Atlantic Commerce, Charge Anywhere, Kanoo, SunCash, and others.

When selecting an e-commerce option and payment gateway, businesses must consider security, pricing, features, and integration options to help them choose a solution that meets their needs and budget.

The future of e-commerce in The Bahamas looks bright as more businesses embrace the online marketplace. With most Bahamians owning smartphones and access to high-speed internet, mobile commerce is expected to play an increasingly vital role in the e-commerce landscape.

Overall, by leveraging the power of e-commerce, businesses in The Bahamas can expand their reach, boost sales, and enhance the customer experience. As the e-commerce industry continues to evolve, it will be exciting to see how businesses in The Bahamas adapt and grow in this ever-changing digital landscape.

TERMINOLOGIES

Terms	Definition
Abating	The process of becoming less intense or widespread. In business, this term often refers to reducing negative factors, such as costs or risks.
Algorithms	These rules or procedures help organize and rank search results and ads, ensuring everything is in order. They help decide how to show and rank content.
API Integration	The process of enabling separate software applications to communicate with each other via APIs (Application Programming Interfaces). This integration allows different systems to share data and functionality.
Automated Cash	Retail or banking often uses systems or processes that handle cash transactions without human intervention.
Brand Identity	The visible elements of a brand, such as color, design, and logo, which identify and distinguish the brand in consumers' minds.
Bahamian Currency	The legal tender used in The Bahamas, known as the Bahamian Dollar (BSD), is typically tied to the US dollar at a one-to-one ratio.

TERMINOLOGIES

Credit Card	A payment card issued to users as a payment method, allowing the cardholder to pay for goods and services based on the holder's promise to pay for them.
Debit Card	A payment card that deducts money directly from a consumer's checking account to pay for a purchase.
E-wallets	Digital tools that keep your payment details and passwords for many payment methods and websites make it easy and safe to buy things online.
End-to-End Payment	A payment system that manages the entire process, from the sale to putting money in the receiver's account.
Global Market	The international exchange of goods and services transcends national boundaries and cultures.
In-App Advertising	Advertisements that appear within a mobile application. They can be banners, videos, or interactive ads.
Search Engine Optimization (SEO)	The practice of increasing the quantity and quality of traffic to a website through organic search engine results.

Target Customers	A specific group of consumers identified as the recipients of a particular marketing message or campaign.
Upfront Investment	The first amount of money needed to start a project or business.
User Experience	The overall experience of a person using a product, especially regarding how easy or pleasing the product is.
Wholesale Businesses	Companies that sell goods in large quantities at lower prices, typically to retailers or other businesses, rather than directly to consumers.

REFERENCES

Commonwealth of The Bahamas, Ministry of Finance. (2003, January). E-commerce Policy Statement. Retrieved from https://www.bahamas.gov.bs/wps/wcm/connect/71f04e08-4561-4217-ba4d-d4a21f8960b6/EcommercePolicyStatement.pdf?MOD=AJPERES&CACHEID=71f04e08-4561-4217-ba4d-d4a21f8960b

CBRE. (2022, May 16). How High Will E-Commerce Sales Go? Retrieved from https://www.cbre.com/insights/articles/omnichannel-how-high-will-e-commerce-sales-go

Central Bank of The Bahamas. (2021). 2020 CBOB Annual Report. Retrieved from https://cdn.centralbankbahamas.com/documents/2021-05-05-14-14-43-2020-CBOB-Annual-Report.pdf

Central Bank of The Bahamas. (2023). 2022 CBOB Annual Report and Financial Statements. Retrieved from https://www.centralbankbahamas.com/viewPDF/documents/2023-05-09-12-27-39-2022-CB0B-Annual-Report-and-FS.pdf

Coppola, D. (2021, October 13). Global number of digital buyers 2014-2021. Statista. Retrieved January 18, 2023, from https://www.statista.com/statistics/251666/number-of-digital-buyers-worldwide/

Kemp, S. (2022, February 15). Digital 2022: The Bahamas. In Digital 2022: Local Country Headlines Report. Retrieved from https://datareportal.com/reports/digital-2022-bahamas

PCI Security Standards Council. (2018, July). PCI DSS Quick Reference Guide: Understanding the Payment Card Industry Data Security Standard version 3.2.1. Retrieved from https://listings.pcisecuritystandards.org/documents/PCI_DSS-QRG-v3_2_1.pdf

REFERENCES

DataReportal. (2022). Digital 2022: The Bahamas. Retrieved from https://datareportal.com/reports/digital-2022-bahamas

DataReportal. (2023). Digital 2023: The Bahamas. Retrieved from https://datareportal.com/reports/digital-2023-bahamas

Silicon Caribe. (2023, February 10). Key Trends Shaping Caribbean e-Commerce in 2023. Retrieved from https://www.siliconcaribe.com/2023/02/10/key-trends-shaping-caribbean-e-commerce-in-2023/

Chambers and Partners. (2023). Banking & Finance 2023 - Bahamas. Retrieved from https://practiceguides.chambers.com/practice-guides/banking-finance-2023/bahamas/trends-and-developments

U.S. Commercial Service. (n.d.). Bahamas - Country Commercial Guide. Retrieved from https://www.trade.gov/country-commercial-guides/bahamas-ecommerce

Privacy Shield Framework. (n.d.). Bahamas – eCommerce. Retrieved from https://www.privacyshield.gov/ps/article?id=Bahamas-eCommerce

McKinsey & Company. (2023). The 2023 McKinsey Global Payments Report. Retrieved from https://www.mckinsey.com/industries/financial-services/our-insights/the-2023-mckinsey-global-payments-report

Bahamas Department of Inland Revenue. (2023). Business License Act, 2023. Retrieved from https://inlandrevenue.finance.gov.bs/wp-content/uploads/2023/07/Business-Licence-Act-2023.pdf

Central Bank of The Bahamas. (n.d.). Payment Providers. Retrieved from https://www.centralbankbahamas.com/bank-supervision/payment-providers

Eyewitness News Bahamas. (n.d.). Island Pay's Digital Payment Opportunities in The Bahamas. Retrieved from https://ewnews.com/island-pay-banking-shift-to-provide-significant-opportunities-in-digital-payment-space

REFERENCES

J.P. Morgan. (2023). Key Payment Trends for 2023. Retrieved from https://www.jpmorgan.com/insights/payments/payment-trends/five-payment-trends-in-2023

Central Bank of The Bahamas. (n.d.). Press Release: Public Update on The Bahamas Digital Currency SandDollar. Retrieved from https://www.centralbankbahamas.com/news/press-releases/press-release-public-update-on-the-bahamas-digital-currency-sanddollar-1

Capgemini. (2023). Top Trends in Payments 2023. Retrieved from https://www.capgemini.com/insights/research-library/top-trends-in-payments-2023/

Unnax. (2023). Digital Payment Trends for 2023. Retrieved from https://www.unnax.com/payment-trends-2023/

Host Merchant Services. (2023, August). Digital Payment Trends 2023. Retrieved from https://www.hostmerchantservices.com/2023/08/digital-payment-trends-2023/

Royal Bank of Canada. (n.d.). Ecommerce Solutions - Royal Bank. Retrieved from http://www.rbcroyalbank.com/caribbean/bahamas/business/merchant-services/ecommerce-solutions.html

First Atlantic Commerce. (n.d.). Bahamas Banks that work with First Atlantic Commerce. Retrieved from https://firstatlanticcommerce.com/blog-fac/bahamas-banks-that-work-with-first-atlantic-commerce/

Bank of the Bahamas Limited. (n.d.). Merchant Services. Retrieved from https://www.bankbahamas.com/merchant-services

Bahamas Ministry of Finance. (n.d.). Retrieved from https://www.bahamas.gov.bs/finance/

REFERENCES

DLA Piper. (n.d.). Bahamas Data Protection Act. Retrieved from https://www.dlapiperdataprotection.com/system/modules/za.co.heliosdesign.dla.lotw.data_protection/functions/handbook.pdf?country-1=BS

Grand View Research. (2023). Global Payment Gateway Market Report 2023. Retrieved from https://www.grandviewresearch.com/press-release/global-digital-payments-market

ABOUT THE AUTHOR

C. Stephan Brown, an e-commerce expert with over nine years of experience in the field, is the visionary behind CSB Tech Emporium. He is a Bahamian software leader known for his bespoke web and mobile applications.

CSB Tech Emporium is a team focused on developing practical solutions tailored for various businesses, from emerging startups to established companies.

Stephan's approach is straightforward: he blends his technical skills with a practical understanding of business needs. With a foundation in applications programming and business administration, Stephan has a well-rounded perspective on the intricacies of online commerce.

In his book, "Cracking the E-Commerce Code, The Bahamas," he shares insights from his journey and the lessons learned at CSB Tech Emporium. The book offers straightforward strategies for those looking to navigate the realms of e-commerce and m-commerce effectively.

Designed with entrepreneurs and seasoned business owners in mind, the book provides Stephan's down-to-earth advice, drawing from the lively tech scene in The Bahamas. It's meant to be a practical guide for anyone interested in making their mark in the digital business world.

Stephan aims to bridge the gap between technical know-how and business savvy, giving readers an accessible look into online business. He distills the essence of CSB Tech's services, which include web development, mobile solutions, and custom software, into practical advice for achieving success in e-commerce.

"Cracking the E-Commerce Code, The Bahamas" is a straightforward, no-nonsense guide for those ready to explore digital innovation and its benefits. Join C. Stephan Brown and CSB Tech Emporium in this journey to develop a successful digital presence.

WHY READ CRACKING THE E-COMMERCE CODE: THE BAHAMAS?

In the rapidly evolving digital landscape, "Cracking the E-Commerce Code: The Bahamas," authored by the accomplished C. Stephan Brown, offers a vital roadmap for navigating the e-commerce sector, particularly in the unique context of The Bahamas. This book, a product of Brown's extensive experience and the innovative spirit of CSB Tech Emporium stands as a crucial resource for anyone looking to make their mark in online business within this region.

The book delves deep into The Bahamas' unique opportunities for digital commerce, shaped by its distinct geographic and economic characteristics. It's a comprehensive guide, moving beyond the basics to provide a detailed understanding of how to succeed in the Bahamian online marketplace. Covering a range of topics, from establishing an online store to leveraging social media and mobile commerce, the guide is packed with practical advice and actionable steps.

What sets this book apart is its relevance to a wide audience. Whether you're a seasoned entrepreneur looking to expand your digital footprint or a newcomer stepping into the online business world, this book offers valuable insights and guidance. It blends Brown's technical expertise and practical business knowledge, making it a reliable starting point for informed decision-making in your business ventures.

WHY READ CRACKING THE E-COMMERCE CODE: THE BAHAMAS?

"Cracking the E-Commerce Code: The Bahamas" is more than a book; it's an invitation to embark on a journey through the dynamic world of e-commerce in a distinctive market. It's a tool that arms readers with the knowledge and skills needed to excel in the digital economy of The Bahamas.

Additionally, for a broader perspective on e-commerce and technology, a visit to the CSB Tech Emporium website is highly beneficial. It provides deeper dive into the intersection of technology and business, reflecting the innovative approach that Brown and his team bring to the digital lands.

Made in the USA
Columbia, SC
09 July 2024

f64d4a4c-c59d-44ef-ab1f-8cf1f3cda85fR01